# Building the Sandcastles of Life

## A Parent's Guide to Psychological Wellbeing for Children

**Fiona Werle**

Cover head shot photo by Emma Braun
Editing and Design Dulci Werle and Moral Support

ISBN 978-0-9944884-0-4
ISBN – 13 9780994488404

Fiona Werle

**Dedicated to my Father and Brother**

**Angels in Heaven**

## About the Author

Fiona Naomi Werle

Fiona is a Mother of four, Wife, Social Scientist and a practicing Sandplay Therapist and Counsellor.

Psychological dilemmas have intrigued Fiona for over three decades, interested in what people do, say, how they act and think. Her philosophy on how to live a meaningful life, a purposeful and honourable life, by being true and authentic, drives her passions. Her ideals would see a flourishing in community and families using originality of thought, where dogmas of others ideals remain just that, another's. What is my purpose in life; this question drove her to read a wide array of philosophy and to look at deep psychology, ecopsychology (environmental influence), existentialism, spiritualism, ancient religions and all to satisfy an innate curiosity about all human lives, past and present. She wonders constantly about the emotions and motives behind what people do, young and old. She will always wonder just as much about herself.

She studied Social Science later in life in search of meaning for her lifelong research into the human psyche. The death of her brother in her 30's was the catalyst to delve deep into the mystery surrounding death and dying. Here she found solace in the Tibetan Book of the Living and Dying and from there she renewed her faith in the ideals of spiritualism and her intimate contact with the universe. Two years later her father passed, Fiona realized that his death was surrounded by another realm of realization, that of our worst fears playing out. Her father had always stated that his worst fear was being buried alive, and it was on this day that this very nearly played out. Steeped in esoteric mystery her father's soul had not yet accepted his passing, and her attempts to save her father the excruciating fear of living out his worst nightmare, were met by an innate ability to enact a ritual, unknown previously, untaught, but somehow familiar to send her father to the light.

Thus a new relationship began with her sense of whom she was, where she came from, and what she was capable of achieving using her innate, inherited and gifted qualities to further her self-growth. She delved into meditation, Mindfulness and self-discovery using ancient text, inner wisdom and the experience of life. She studied Positive psychology and wellbeing and found that Sandplay Technique was the tool which applied all of the resources and reached the depths of the unconscious mind and allowed her to see, feel and know what she had always suspected, that as individuals we all hold the key to our own self-growth and development.

Fiona lived for a good part of her life in Europe, where she furthered her study in Feng Shui, travelled extensively through England, Scotland, Ireland, Cyprus, Italy, Germany, Switzerland, Austria, France, Spain, Portugal, Malta, Belgium, Luxemburg and Hungary where her father's roots were planted. Her travels to America took her to New York and down the East Coast through North and South Carolina.

In her last years of living in Europe, Fiona hosted a radio program, the only English speaking talk back radio show in Holland. The topics were always around her guests and their inner thoughts and emotions, where she gently offered a platform for a variety of guests to talk about their passions, wants, likes and dislikes.

Fiona is an Expert on Parenting and Family Relationships. Her training, keynote speaking and workshops are interesting and filled with knowledge and insight.

## Table of Contents

# *Introduction*

*Counselling is a philosophy of wellness it allows the therapist to look at the individual and think what is the best process for this person, what will get them to good psychological health in the quickest way, where all taught skills will be of a lifelong benefit, leading toward new sources of learning, growth and self-development*

We often project onto others what we need to see for our own learning. We've all heard people saying others are mirror images. The lessons we learn, sometimes successfully, sometimes not so, are played out in our private playgrounds in which we learn and grow; birth, school, separation, trauma, becoming a parent for the first time, all this changes our lives dramatically, the loss of a loved one can take our emotions to places we never knew existed, then at later stages in life we may experience financial difficulties, social issues, changing family dynamics. As we get older we look for a sense of connection, some choose to ground their faith in religion others go deep into their psyche and explore their soul-equation in search for answers.

This book is a guide for those who want to explore this in others, however, as we know we cannot even begin to understand another until we fully know ourselves. The pages that follow will guide you through processes, all thought provoking, but the underlying concept is that of the stages of development and achieving self-growth and good psychological health and wellness.

We attract what we put out, law of attraction 101 and those we choose as partners, lovers, or friends become our best teachers. The people in our immediate circle push our buttons and become mirror images of what we don't like about ourselves and for better or worse our best teachers! These are the very people who helped us to make our self-equation. So next time someone pushes your buttons, be grateful for the lesson!

Consider for a moment, that your life consists of a multitude of memories. Think about your childhood and all those memories. Now look at you as an adult. Do you hear yourself saying things, repeating your parent's words as they echo: "You can't do that, you're too short, too tall, too thin, too fat, too dumb, that's a boys job, girls can't do that" and on it goes – all these words we took in to our being, they formed part of our belief system and those words were stored in our unconscious mind, whose attached emotions are warehoused in the very cells of our body. This concept forms a part of the theory of psychosomatics, which is a very real area of health and wellness in which unhappy people will undoubtedly create or manifest pain within the body. This is the body mind connection; it is how our system communicates to us that there is a dis-ease building up, which deals normally with an issue left unchecked.

Do you get a headache at the mention of someone's name or a task? Do you feel sick in your stomach from nerves if you have to do public speaking? Does your ankle hurt when you need to step up, move forward, and take control? This is your body reacting, saying *"no I can't do it, I won't do it, you told me I couldn't, shouldn't!"* You get the picture; our resistance is entirely stored within us. This is the mind body connection. This is the depth at which the child ego pushed down the hurts and pains in order to protect us. It served us then, but as adults, it no longer serves to hold the pains of yesteryear.

Left unchecked this stagnation can erupt into dis-ease, illness or even death in extreme cases, because it was easier to manifest cancer or heartache, than to look at the issue that has caused you so much discomfort. This is the power of psychosomatics. No issue, no disease! Harsh words, yes, but I want to show you that you have more control over your Self-Equation than you think you do.

And here's why; as adults, capable of change, growth, wisdom and knowledge we still sit with our deep seated beliefs (think the iceberg effect) where the traumas are pushed down into the unseen realm, this is your unconscious mind. Only a small part of our true self is exposed to the outer world, the conscious aspect which is functional a mere 5-10% of the time. On average we function more from this unseen realm, the unconscious mind 90-95% of the time. This is the nagging voice in your head, rumination, the monkey mind, the wounded ego, the one that confirms to you as an adult that 'No you can't do that, remember!', and so we don't! We have our conscious mind, subconscious and then our unconscious mind, this is where deep psychology is found and this is where we work in Counselling using Sandplay Technique, Mindfulness and other valuable counselling skills, to work through those childhood traumas that are still affecting behaviour to this day.

Mindfulness allows us to be present here and now in the moment of the self-equation. Sandplay pieces represent fragments in a time, stored in a memory, where you pushed your emotions down in order to cope in dealing with a situation or a person's behaviour towards you as a child. Much like in the movie 'Inside Out', where the different coloured marbles represented different memories. The ego at the time will sort memories into categories; however, what the ego deemed as a red marble, an angry memory, may now have changed as you change your perception around people, places and experiences. This is the job of the ego; however, what we need is a healthy balance and that is why presenting issues to the Sandtray can open up that deep part of our inner self and gently allows an exploration into our self-equation.

Mindfulness helps to ease the burdens of the mind, to relax the inner thinking to allow a space, peace and tranquility to enter. Once you have mastered Mindfulness you will be amazed at the change in your overall health and wellbeing. You will remember to breath, to smell the roses, to see that with every situation, challenge and cross road that you have a conscious choice.

I am here to let you know you CAN steer your own ship and yes there will always be a strong wind blowing you off course, dangerous undercurrents and rips, shark infested waters, but isn't this a wonderful metaphor for life, because on the other hand you will also experience perfect sun filled days, calm waters, gentle breeze, dolphins playing and sails billowing in the gentle breeze.

Here you see two polar opposites, duality, and a shadow side neither can exist without the other. The more you experience adversity with an open mind the more you get to know the many sides of you. The more you relax into the joy of profound synchronicity the more you attract good health and wellness to YOU. The key is self-awareness and the courage to climb from the depths of self-indifference to the heights of self-awareness.

Carl Jung the famous Psychoanalyst who worked alongside Freud, was significant in the evolution of Sandplay, he would have loved our modern day Star Wars and all the archetypes, the fusion between fantasy, reality, the present and the past and the person we perceive ourselves to be and our shadow self! I mean who doesn't want to be the hero or heroine in their own story?

The rest is how we got to be the characters in our life's story. Just like our dream state, we are each and every character or piece in the sand picture, our unconscious mind playing out our unresolved issues, childhood traumas, leading us to the experiential centre of 'who am I?' and 'what is my purpose?'

Counselling allows just that, opening up our inner psyche to place within the boundaries of the Sandtray the story of our childhood. This is where we get to see the patterns of our parents, grandparents and forefathers/mothers. Here we can see if a significant other was a threat to us in our childhood, such as it is now the case with many victims of childhood sexual abuse – their memory has been triggered by another's story, or seeing the abusers on TV. We use images, memory and story to get to the heart of the real issue, and allow the pain stored in the cells of the body to release. The event will never go away, nor will the memory; however, the pain can be eased.

Once here, Sandplay allows clients to step back and look at dysfunctional behaviour, set patterns and beliefs, for example are you one of those people who just never finishes anything, could it be, you were told by your father that you would never amount to anything in life, so what do you do? You proved him right, that's how you showed your love. Or are you a high achiever, yet your mother thinks you can still do better.

If you attract the wrong type of man into your life, you know the sort I mean, he's just not the right person for you - you may develop a low self-esteem, why? This was a pattern you set up as a child to get attention from your father. If you have as your mantra – "oh I can't do it" and now you believe you can't do anything, not even attract a partner that you desire or who desires you. In effect you have the law of attraction working against you, reverse this by changing your thinking and you attract positivity.

You may have sexual issues, perhaps you were brought up to be a good Catholic girl and told that, feelings of sexual desire were bad, so you buried them deep within. As a consequence, you may have had psychosomatic issues such as; invisible pregnancies, cancer of the ovaries or miscarriages. So be careful of what you are reading here, I am not saying that there wasn't a legitimate physical reason why you had problems, however, look at what we have already covered in this section around our cells holding memory and psychosomatics. Tapping into what actually set that idea into the mind of the child can set you free. Sex is good, good sex is great! No church religion or state can tell an adult what to do with your body or your urges. As you listen to your mind listen to your body also, it's speaking to you.

As a Sandplay practitioner I watch your body language and listen to your verbal language; with adults I listen for any incongruences, such as you saying, "I'm so sad", with a smile on your face. What's going on there? Once we narrow down a current issue, then I ask you to place that issue in the Sandtray, that's where things start getting interesting.

With the kids in Sandplay it's a little different, they will choose their pieces and do their own processing in the tray, they do this by moving the pieces around, burying pieces in the sand, placing pieces together, boys in particular will have fighting battle scenes, girls in general tend to like fairy-tale archetypes. The idea is, they are working through issues from the unconscious, whether it is dealing with how parents argue often or the birth of a new sibling or more traumatic issues. Children use the Sandtray as a place of therapy, of sorting through the self-equation thereby releasing pent-up stress held in their body.

Carl Jung in his little red book talks a lot about our 'other selves', he shows us how we can be many personalities in one and I don't mean schizophrenia, I am talking about archetypes, characters that we have as traits, such as the Rescuer, the Martyr, the Leader, the Enabler, these traits are found within our psyche, they make up parts of our personality.

Tapping into character traits is what make us all unique, although some traits have been adopted from our parents and because of this some children lose their own sense of identity. The key is to be aware of your personality traits, recognise them, as many as possible and find the balance. It's important that if you are a rescuer, you allow yourself to be rescued or if you are a martyr you recognise that you can't always save the world.

This is what the Sandtray will reveal through the chosen figurines and other pieces placed seemingly randomly in the tray. This is your story! The story of your inner child, I am a reader and as I read I will be curious and ask questions, only you know the answers. Your unconscious is what drives most of your waking hours, and well into sleep, so it is necessary to tap into this vast iceberg in order to find the essence of you. Buried very deep beneath the ocean lies the true you, ready to be revealed and swim to the surface to finally begin to live a true authentic life, just as Mother Nature intended.

As a therapist, I have schooled in many different models of therapy, and had some great teachers along the way. Some techniques I use are Cognitive Behavioural Therapy (CBT) Rational Emotive Behavioural Therapy (REBT), Person Centred, Mindfulness, Positive Psychology and Sandplay Technique. It was when I started learning the latter, Sandplay, that I realised I had found my calling, it was aligning to every other discipline and philosophy I adhered too. Sandplay Technique was the glue.

Although I must confess, there are many more therapeutic models to add to my skill set, these are the ones I turn to on a regular basis. Within each one of these models in turn, there can be found another layer of skills, such as tentative listening, being congruent, non-judgmental, being in the here and now, challenging, normalising and within that there are the subtleties of observing body language, listening to see if the story is consistent with the person's emotions, meaning; if he or she is telling a story of fear and deceit, I would look at the body language, is she smiling, sad, animated or talking fast?

As part of the road to resilience, I look for roadblocks, resistance or resentment, this gives clues to the mind of the person in therapy, the overall picture indicates to me where the person stands on a scale of 1 – 10 in their level of mental health or I prefer the term psychological wellbeing. Scaling is a great method to use with loved ones at home if they are feeling unwell, unhappy or just plain out of sorts, using the scaling method allows you to view a snap shot where the person is here and now. It would be a good tool for couples to use, may be of benefit also with work colleagues.

It would be wrong if I had not been a part of the above processes as a client. The ideal therapist has preferably, before they open up their practice, had counselling themselves, resolved major issues and is in a place of acceptance. It is advisable that all who are interested in being therapists in whatever capacity, to have experienced their own counselling for many reasons, but the major one is that you cannot walk in another's shoes and show empathy if your mind turns the whole time to your own thoughts, memories and traumas.

It is also important for parents, those who want to be the best they can be for their children to undergo therapy to shift any patterns or beliefs inherited from their own childhood which does not serve them now. The counselling room is not the place for a therapist to resolve their own issues; it is a space to hold your client, a space to discover new perspectives and a place where what is said in the room stays in the room as part of a healthy therapeutic alliance. This relationship is like no other, for with whom can we trust to pour out our heart, to say things that are directed at others and in the same time explore the depths of where these words have sprung and who was involved in the planting of our pain.

I still uncover layers in myself, I am still learning and still discovering that our unique life experience paves the way to greater oceans of depth. As I sit with a client I will tap into an innate intuition to fulfil the question of what method best serves my client today, now, at this moment. Sometimes I may offer the talk therapy of CBT or REBT, at other times I can help relieve their stress by teaching Mindfulness relaxation techniques. If I feel a client is at the bottom end of the scale, I will prop him or her up by recommending they complete a character strength assessment. This aspect of positive psychology and wellness, a sixty (60) question assessment is a wonderful way for clients to see that they truly do have good qualities to draw on in order to move forward in their healing process.

The most rewarding method that I often draw on is Sandplay Technique. I love the ease at which the pieces in the tray become the pictures the unconscious mind has drawn; how this picture then awakens a part of the clients psyche and nudges them on to discover more, to go deeper, to reawaken a knowing and awareness that resides within us all. The Sandplay Technique knows no language barrier; it cares not if you are culturally different, if you speak a language other than English, nor worship a God different to another. Sandplay Technique cares not your age, you can be 4 or 104 it does not matter.

What matters is that this method enables choice, resilience, awareness, perspective and it opens up your mind to other ways of being. Within these pages I have brought together knowledge from all manner of places in the hope that each and every individual may find something that resonates with your soul, some truth or knowledge that you can tap into and use as a base to further your learning.

This book is showing you that you too, can bring into your life some elements to use as therapy. As we will see in this book, younger children benefit by simply being able to play out their childhood issues in the sand box. Wouldn't it be great though if every child care centre the knowledge of Sandplay Technique?

I have laid down no boundaries with this book as I want to speak to you all, as diverse as you are. I want to show you the universe, to point out to you that we are all from different places, with different values, beliefs and yet each and every one of you can go into the Sandtray and create your picture, your unique life story using your memories, your parent's memories and those of your ancestors tapping into a collective unconscious.

For some, you will be drawn to the stars, astrology, mythology or the ancient scripts of our ancient ancestors who wrote on stone, scrolls and later in books to set out guidelines on how to live a good life, how to be a kind and loving soul. For in the end that is what all humans have in common, we all want to love and be loved.

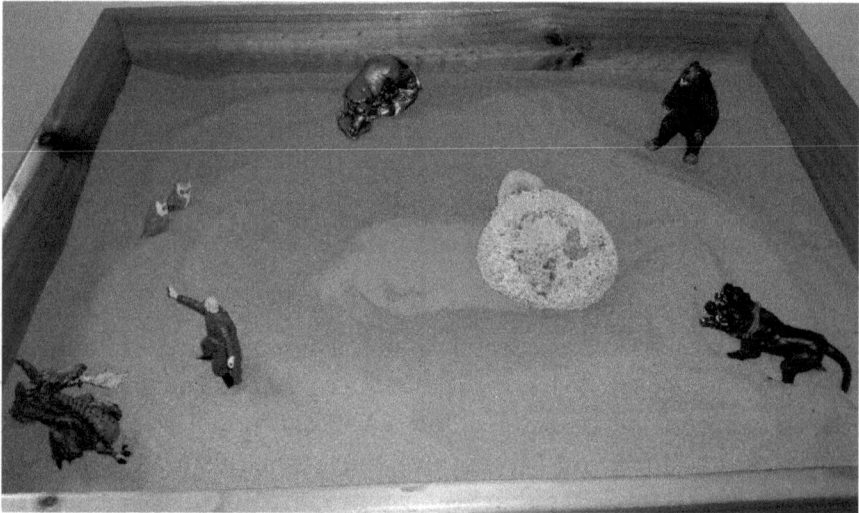

An example of a Sandplay with fire breathing dragon, three headed dog, bear, tiger, hero, 2 owls and in the centre a shell representing the mother or womb. This client has issues around the mother child bonding.

Fiona Werle

# *The Philosophy of Counselling and Sandplay Technique*

---

*We all have the ability to see the past, what
we see determines our future, for all todays
will soon be yesterday.*

---

Sandplay is a psychotherapeutic approach to counselling, this simply means a form of psychology or working with the mind to attain good health and wellbeing. It is a method used for attaining personal development and self-growth. The technique of Sandplay was originated by Margaret Frances Jane Lowenfeld, originally known as the Lowenfeld World Technique. Dora Kalff, who was the neighbour of Carl Jung, studied with Margaret Lowenfeld; she made some links between the deep psychology and inner psychic processes of individuation as spoken of by Carl Jung which then lead her to creating the current method of Sandplay. It was here that a wonderful relationship began between two extremely intelligent, intuitive and deep souls in the analysis and study of depth psychology, Jung and Kalff. Kalff then created her own unique method called Sandplay.

The idea behind the Sandplay method lies in the figurines or images representing a deep psychological meaning or memory for the individual. Images are archetypal, the archetypes hold meaning and emotions. The term archetype has its origins in the ancient Greek words *archein*, which means original or old; and *typos*, which means pattern or model. The combined meaning of archetype is original pattern, of which all other similar persons, objects, or concepts are derived, copied, modelled, or emulated.

Carl Jung coined the concept of archetypes in his theory of the human psyche, he believed that; *universal, mythic characters and archetypes, reside within the collective unconscious of all people. Archetypes represent fundamental human motifs of our experiences as we evolved, they evoke deep emotions.* Although there are many different archetypes, Jung defined twelve primary types that symbolise basic human motivations. Each type has its own set of values, meanings and personality traits.

Most, if not all, people have several archetypes at play in their own self-equation however, one archetype tends to dominate the personality in general. It can be helpful to know which archetypes are at play in oneself and others, especially loved ones, friends and co-workers, in order to gain personal insight into behaviours and motivations of others.

These archetypes or images will show up in the Sandtray and become a part of the sand picture. It is at this point that you will be able to determine whether your child is able to grasp the depth at which their psyche has presented their issue in the form of one or two archetypes.

When you or your child are truly ready for self-growth, the more open you are to other cultures, beliefs, the more you will be able to guide your child to the archetypes and the message they are bringing to the conscious mind. The archetypes are the bridge between the unconscious and the conscious mind, the allowing of this process is a trigger to the mind to open up and begin the journey down into the depth, with the intent of promoting transcendence or self-growth through conscious awareness and then acceptance.

So what follows may be a very different perspective to what you call normal, but what is normal and who says that this visible world is all that there is, what about the invisible? What about energy, magnetism, attraction, intuition, gut instinct and a sense of knowing, these are all invisible senses, unseen yet felt. When you read about fairies, or see the symbols, be open to how your body reacts, if a child reaches for a piece and has an emotional reaction, talk about this there and then; what just happened? Where are you feeling it? Do you feel something in your stomach? As adults we need to be mindful and ask the question; do you automatically reject the truth as myth or Fairy-tales being real? Be mindful, be open minded and enjoy a new perspective.

Allow yourself to view dreams, ecopsychology, culture, myth, fairytales, and ancient languages and ritual as an integral part of who our forefathers/mothers were. I see this with a wide perspective, perhaps even wider knowing that my forefathers were from the ancient line of the Magyars, whose spoken language in itself stands alone as a Uralic language.

Uralic languages all descended from a Proto-Uralic language that existed 7,000 to 10,000 years ago. The Uralic language is the official language of Hungary. This ancient language introduces the significance of symbols, letters and then onto sound and resonance. Basically what I introduce to you is a very wide range of ideas and observations. As a part of my self-equation this ancient Uralic language ties it all into my own meaning making, family and my place in this big wide world.

I have created a Polarity of Balance Model on which can be placed the diverseness of character traits, environmental influences and self. It gives you some idea when creating it either for yourself, a child or a family member as a snap shot of where he or she has been, remember, the past makes the present. Looking at this can help to guide you gently towards seeing the wider perspectives that make up our uniqueness. We are all a sum of our parents, environment and our past.

Put differently when I hear the Hungarian language it brings up emotions in me, it makes me remember good food, nurturing and happy days. My mind has organised this memory association within the positive experiences remembered by my body mind, the trigger which is the language make us feel happy and this is because of childhood memories stored in my unconscious, all directly related to my Hungarian grandmother. Our bond connection, the result of unconditional love, the food, and the nurturing formed this connection and releasing the memory takes me to the past and makes my here and now experience a positive one.

As parents this is the ultimate relationship we can aim for, planting seeds of good memories, feelings of unconditional love so that when our children grow they too can tap into past memories to create a positive here and now experience. This positive role modelling can be passed down from generation to generation, and what a wonderful legacy to leave our future generations.

The philosophy of Counselling and Sandplay holds the key to being able to process memories that stored moments in time that were troubling or traumatic for the child by encouraging a wider perspective, asking the question why? How? Where? By looking at the past, to see how it influences our today.

The memory becomes a part of the unconscious mind, the 90 – 95%. Memory is also stored in the cells of our body, if an event was traumatic this cell is in trauma and is the beginning of any dis-ease it all starts with a cellular imbalance. Triggers, such as poor psychological health, poor diet and nutrition and or unstable environment can cause these primitive cells to mutate. Releasing the memory through Sandplay Technique is a preventative means of psychological health and wellbeing.

Indeed it is this synchronicity of inner and meaning that brings events together in a meaningful connection in the sandtray; thinking of an issue, leads to choosing seemingly random pieces or figurines that represent an archetype, giving the symbolic meaning as represented by our subconscious.

When we write a thought, our brain converts the words – which are symbols – into movements of the fingers and hands, as I am doing now. My thoughts are a direct result of my life's experiences modeled and remodeled to form the views I now hold.

Our unconscious mind is attuned to our surroundings, whether this be our group, society in general and feeling an integral part of the global community or in fact a part of the universe. It is within these aspects our self-symbol can be found. Animals can represent our instinctive nature and the connection with our surroundings.

Take a look at your environment, are you privy to sounds of the early morning calls of the birds, perhaps you have a cat who awakens you in the mornings with her purring and gestures of love and affection. Do you have a loyal dog who you know will stand by you no matter. Look at your surroundings, listen, see, smell, taste and connect intuitively.

Our conscious mind continually creates the illusion of a clear formation of an outer world that can hinder the development of our perceptions, which in turn gives rise to burying deeply our instinctual feelings spiritual and psychic self-knowing. This unbalance leads to a severing of our connection to our psychic environment.

Remember when John Smith in Pocahontas could actually hear the animals talking to him. He found himself connected to his eco-environment, which opened up his invisible connections to Mother Earth and her creatures. Opening up results in a softening, in this softening we can hear the subliminal messages, whispers in the winds, answers to our questions. A balance to body mind and soul is key to understanding the symbols that we find all around us.

When we speak, our brain converts a sequence of symbols – the letters and words of thought, into a sequence of movements made by our tongue and lip muscles. The brain stores the memory and the body holds the emotion associated with the memory. I know that I am tainted with the ghosts of my parents beliefs. Their seeds lying within me, in wait of further nurturing. Sometimes I water these seeds and am astonished at the awareness of that.

So within me, as in you, lays your parents ever presence, ready to surface to control your every thought. Allow this to occur with a knowing that they are only there as guides, for better or worse. If good seeds have been planted by your parents you will in turn plant good seeds in your child and they will flourish. We all carry around with us our inner child.

# Where It All Begins - The Memory

*The other day upon the stair I saw a man who wasn't there, he wasn't there again today, how I wish he'd go away.*

*Anon*

What are memories and do we all have them? Everything that has ever happened to you is recorded in the form of a memory. We have two types of memory; Implicit and Explicit. Our implicit memory begins at conception, as the brain is forming the fetus stores the memories in the form of the sound of a significant others voice, the mother, music or an act. These are the memories that are stored in the babies' unconscious mind, it forms the basis of who we are, and who and what we attract, our expectations of the world, our conditioning is formed by these early experiences. The unconscious mind is where the bulk of the processing and conditioning forms about 90%.

Explicit memory is formed as a part of our conscious mind, it enables us to make sense of the past. This area of conscious mind and explicit memory forms only about 10% of awareness.

The coming together of the implicit and explicit memory, the conscious and unconscious mind occurs in the area of the brain known as the hippocampus. This is the engine room that makes sense of images, emotions and sensations. It is done by way of images or pictures that make up our explicit understanding of our past experiences.

Sandplay in its unique form is able to re-produce the working of this process whereby the memory, through the Sandtray pieces, integrates both memories and the sand picture which allows this bringing together of the elements that makes up our complex system of thought processes; past hurt feelings, emotions, abstract, intuition, instinct, patterns, connections, death, hopes, dreams, conscious movement, fantasy, unknown, spiritual, intents, family systems and core personality can all appear.

The pictures or images we use when we store our memories translate in the form of archetypes and symbols. Each archetype and symbol will be unique to each individual and their experiences of life. Each memory is associated with an emotion, like fear, anger, depression, anxiety, resentment, despair and shame as negative emotions or joy, bliss, trust, initiative or courage as positive emotions. When placing the pieces in the tray you are placing emotions represented by an image. The key is to re-awaken your implicit memory so that your explicit memory can consciously recognise past experience and make sense of these moments in time. These are the archetypes, symbols, emotions, family systems, environmental influences, character traits, conditioning and behaviours that make up the Polarity of Balance.

The Polarity of Balance Model allows us to see that our self-equation is made up of experiences, emotions and patterns; these can all be experienced at the polar ends of the self-equation. Yet without experiencing the extremes, it is difficult to find our true centre of balance. The model also suggests that this movement is in constant motion, which allows the individual to move towards self-development.

Fiona Werle

# Polarity and the Benefits in the Child's Development

---

*Creative living is all about the tension
between the two poles, you can't stay in
either extreme, but you need to travel there
to find the balance.*

---

Within the process of counselling the polarities of the mind can tilt in favour of the deepest unknowing reaching into areas that touch on insanity, we have all been there whether we can admit this or not, yet having been there allows you to know it, feel it, live it and then choose to let it go. Sitting at this end of the polarity serves a purpose, only once you have experienced the depth of darkness, the great void, do you really understand the agony of stepping out, one step at a time and making sure not to slide too quickly to the extreme which is ecstasy. Only to find this was short lived, so back you go.

Each movement in the process, the depth of the movement is lessened by previous visits. It is all about getting the balance right and like a pendulum you swing from side to side, ever moving in a momentum that seems to have life and cause of its own. You are pushed along and at each junction there is a lesson, a learning, or an epiphany, a brief meeting with the inner child, you are swung in another perpetual motion to the other side, perhaps this is consciousness awaking and it is here that you consolidate the learning, check for reactions, responses or road blocks.

Till once more the motion drives us back towards the depths of our being; our unconscious, where we find ourselves back in the past, where trauma resides, experience sits and making sense of chance encounters, family acts and the equation of self in all this turmoil of emotion brings us to feelings of deep emotion and anguish.

On it goes, that perpetual swing from one end of the pole to the other, forming as it goes our self-equation, the changes aligned with the movements of our self-discovery. At each junction we are building resilience, our self-awareness is unfolding. Sandplay allows a glimpse into this motion: in and out, seen and unseen, visible and invisible. The pieces in the Sandtray are our forbearers speaking to us, wanting us to heal, to break the chain of ancestral wounds and family patterns. It is a place of letting go, a place where ego, soul, body and mind come to an understanding. It is a releasing of memories, of the pain that held those memories alive and the emotions behind the pain. All stored deeply within our body's cells and deep down in our unconscious mind.

The letting go must adhere to the self-equation, all parts must be in alignment for the process to work properly. This is no place for our rational mind alone, yet it is the rational mind that allows, encourages even, the moment of being in the present, the here and now, and the emptying of space, that can then be filled with the knowing of the inner psyche that acts as the collector of the stored memory and brings forth a new awareness.

Allowing, giving over and trusting in the process are the pre-requisites for a spontaneous healing in the Sandtray. When parents understand that the importance of a healthy relationship with their child is influenced by the polarity experienced by the parent, then the process is empowering for both parent and child. Any question about blame is then put aside, any negativity can then be viewed from a new perspective and the Polarity of Balance becomes a snap shot into our own and our Childs self-development.

# Polarity of Balance Model

## Movements in the Self-Equation

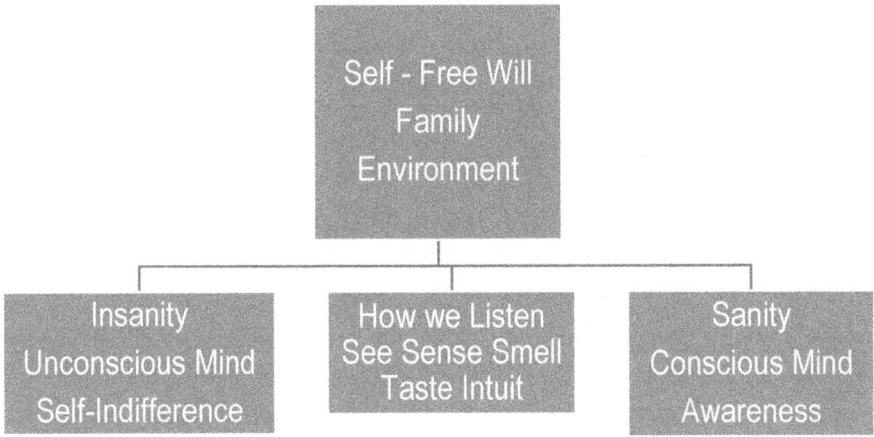

Self - Free Will
Family
Environment

| Insanity Unconscious Mind Self-Indifference | How we Listen See Sense Smell Taste Intuit | Sanity Conscious Mind Awareness |

| | |
|---|---|
| Resistance | Resilience |
| Illness | Health |
| Mistrust | Trust |
| Shame | Autonomy |
| Guilt | Initiative |
| Inferiority | Industry |
| Isolation | Intimacy |
| Stagnation | Growth |
| Despair | Integrity |
| Doubt | Courage |
| Hatred | Love |

# *Looking at Your Inner Child*

*You can't always be there to stop kids falling,
but you can be there to pick them up, dust
them off and send them on their way again*

As children we were carried away in a world of fantasy and fiction living in our imaginations – flying in the air, soaring through the sky, at home in the trees, caves and wonderlands. We were talking to the animals, listening to the whispers of the wind. We were dancing with our souls. As Jung said, *"the living meaning only lives when we experience it in and through ourselves"*. Our childhood self-explorations are the key to our psychological understanding of ourselves and help towards finding our meaning in life. These childhood explorations are our connection with past and present, a bridge to further developmental stages.

If at any point this bridge collapses, then the severing of self occurs. There is no longer the means by which to explore the deep unconscious, soul or inner self and thus a dis-connection occurs in the thinking process. This imbalance is often a symptom of mental illness, but only as viewed in Western psychology. For Jung, insanity was not regarded as something completely set apart from sanity, but rather as lying on the extreme ends of the spectrum, polar opposites. It is for this reason I have included it on the Polarity of Balance. In order to experience ecstasy one needs to also experience depression to fully know the feelings and behaviour associated with going into the depths and extremes of these emotional states. Only then can there be a harmony in the mind body experience as we make movements along the Polarity of Balance.

A child, you may think has not lived long enough to have had enough experiences to create their Polarity of Balance, yet when we set out a model for a child we integrate the whole family, the conception, gestation, the birth, the home, environment and community. Therefore, even a newborn baby has its own self-equation.

Where on this equation is the child shaped? The questions; who am I, where do I belong, what is my purpose? A child is forming an identity, being conditioned and storing memories from a very early age. They may not consciously be asking the Socratic questions of life, however this Socratic form of questioning highlights our genuine need to merge the conscious mind with the unconscious.

Children at any age can experience extreme polarities like birth, death, sanity, insanity, depression, and ecstasy, which all combine to shape how they view and understand their world. A newborn baby of a drug addicted mother will already have an implicit memory of this and a different experience of life at birth than that of a healthy baby mother bond.

Sandplay enables a snapshot into a part of this equation. Placing depression into the Sandtray can highlight joy which without this movement may have seemed illusive, unapproachable even. Within the Sandtray magic occurs, you begin to engage in a self-explorative activity, psychological investigation into your own or your child's self –equation. Simply by placing pieces as symbols into the Sandtray permitting fantasy and allowing the mind to tap into myth, fairy-tale and memories, the mind opens up. It is in this space you speak to your soul *"the soul in the primitive sense, anima"* -Jung.

As individuals, a child's need to be authentic is caught up

in being in a partnership with parents, family, community, and for teenagers in the wider world. Within this spectrum, children are shaped and it is important that as an individual they are living their true potential and not being the self that carries on familial, dysfunctional or harmful beliefs.

What the child needs in order for good psychological health and wellness is balance. Children are shaped by their parents and significant others. Below is an example of a child who is very in touch with his psychic ability, his inner treasure, he has been told by a teacher that intuition or psychic ability is non-existent, he is denied the ability or permission to use an integral part of his innate psyche. He now feels a need to hide this ability from the outside world, to retain this talent the unconscious mind has buried this ability and the boy is now guarded. His parents relationship is in turmoil, this will affect his childhood development.

Role models need to be very careful when placing their values on children. Our children are different to ourselves, children of this new age are much more in tune with nature, spirit and the invisible world. As we have seen from our young boy who had been encouraged by his mother to use his psychic abilities, his outer world, his school, had different ideas. This child is confused and the wonderful gift of high intuition that should be nurtured and highlighted as a strength, has been literally locked away in a chest and buried. He is burying a part of himself.

This child also has a problem of not going to the toilet, he chooses instead to pooh in his pants. It is interesting to note that at the time his parents were fighting he was at the age of what Freud called the Anal Stage. Below is an outline of this period.

*The anal stage, in Freudian psychology, is the period of human development occurring at about one to three years of age. Around this age, the child begins to toilet train, which brings about the child's fascination in the erogenous zone of the anus. The erogenous zone is focused on the bowel and bladder control. The anal stage coincides with the start of the child's ability to control their anal sphincter, and therefore their ability to pass or withhold feces at will. If the children during this stage can overcome the conflict it will result in a sense of accomplishment and independence.*

*A successful completion of this stage depends on how the parents interact with the child while toilet training. If a parent praises the child and gives rewards for using the toilet properly and at the right times then the child will successfully go through the stage. However, if a parent ridicules and punishes a child while he or she is at this stage, the child can respond in negative ways.*

*As mentioned before the ability for the children to be successful in this stage is solely dependent upon their parents and the approach they use towards toilet training. Freud believed that parents should promote the use of toilet training with praise and rewards. The use of positive reinforcement after using the toilet at the appropriate times encourages positive outcomes. This will help reinforce the feeling that the child is capable of controlling their bladder. The parents help make the outcome of this stage a positive experience which in turn will lead to a competent, productive, and creative adult. This stage is also important in the child's future relationships with authority.*

# Positive Parenting and the Child's Wellbeing

*Experience brings harmony and discord to life, yet this is how we experience diversity, just like the seasons we must experience the extremes of hot and cold, dark and light, night and day to feel the rhythms and see the contrast, smell the spring flowers and languish in the green grass of summer. In so doing we use nature as our inspiration, the changes remind us of the transient nature of existence*

In order to understand the effects positive parenting has on your child's wellbeing it is important to first understand that we all have different parenting styles. These styles have been generally classed in the following; Authoritarian, where parents have strict rules, expect their child to be mature and compliant. The next style is Authoritative, where parents are assertive, not restrictive, supportive yet monitor behaviours closely and show clear standards, then we have the Permissive parenting style, these parents rarely discipline, are responsive and allow their child self-regulation. The last style is uninvolved parent, this style speaks for itself and has no place in positive parenting.

When looking at the different styles it is easy to see that if two parents have a differing opinion on which style to use when parenting, this can impact on them showing a united front in parenting, which is key to good positive parenting.

Positive parenting is leading your child towards learning good values and having well rounded beliefs, this is why it is important for parents to unite in their parenting decisions, to share the problem solving, and to us a compatible language. It is a valuable lesson for the child to see and hear that both their parents or carers are able to use positively enforced language, utilize diverse skills to attain a positive outcome and all the while inviting engagement from within the family unit.

A mother with a permissive parenting style can reinforce this unity by never saying yes to a child without first saying, "I'll talk to your dad see what he says and then we can discuss it as a family", because we know otherwise she'll just say, "yes". This allows the permissive styled parent to align their parenting style more to that of the other who may be authoritarian or authoritative and would most likely be saying "No" more often than not.

The role of positive parents is to find a middle ground, as it is here in this important area that mother, father (carers) and child learn to create a dialogue around opinions, where the child learns to see others perspectives and in this way their values are formed. This is the basis of positive parenting and it is a time where parents are experiencing their own interpersonal communication, listening to their own inner voice, which sets us them up for further self- growth and development as adult individuals, as couples and as a family unit.

The greatest benefit to showing a united front as parents, is of course growing healthy children. They will gain the advantage of staying within healthy boundaries and feeling secure in the knowing that both parents share the caring role. This is a healthy family dynamic where parents are the educators, children learn beneficial life skills. Positive parenting builds children who have been given the gift of self-discovery, learning to behave within a social environment and grow to learn intimate aspects of themselves and each family member.

Children who are able to express emotions freely in a positive environment learn to become better leaders and true authentic individuals within the family and society. This is an important element as it allows them to have a dialogue with their inner self, it brings them into the present moment. This is an area of Mindfulness that connects the body and mind, and if a child has been given the ability to use this skill, they can gain an advantage when it comes to self-regulation.

Self-regulation is knowing when you are in a bad place, it teaches the child that if they do something wrong, something outside of their values that stress levels will rise and they may suffer from anxiety. It could begin with a stomach ache; this may be the beginning of regret at what you have done. A positive parenting environment allows the child to experience this as part of self-regulation, knowing that it is all part of the pathway to growing healthy children. A cohesive family is a family that unites together, learns together and grows together yet allowing each individual the opportunity within the interdependent framework in which to explore.

Knowing your place and having a sense of belonging, feeling safe, secure and loved unconditionally is how healthy functioning parents serve their child's wellbeing. These factors all stimulate the child's psychological and biological growth. Nobody however gets away without having to go through the terrible twos, hormonal teenagers or ego driven adolescents. As parents your job is to support them, catch them when they fall, dust them off and send them on their way again. The key is to instill good values, be a positive role model and practice mindful parenting.

When we have healthy thoughts we trigger our body's response by wanting to eat healthy foods, enjoy regular exercise and attract positive relationships. Our positive thoughts give rise to an open conversation with our higher self (spirit) and that aligns our energies to a higher level, this then becomes the realm of law of attraction. When you are in a positive frame of mind you are much more open to new ideas, new people and new possibilities. Our higher self or often called our super conscious mind is a radar, it signals to the mind the infinite opportunities that await.

Positive parenting is a series of methods, skills, attributes, mindsets, internal dialogues and much more. If we as parents can find the balance between mind, body, spirit or thinking, feeling and intuition then the equation leads us to a more balanced way of parenting. This is enough to be called positive parenting, because at the end of the day, we are not super heroes, we are humans with all our baggage, our own emotional states and sometimes we get it wrong, yet those are the moments that determine when we know we got it right.

A happy family needs leaders and part time superheroes, but mostly what a healthy family needs are parents who are willing to show their flaws, their emotions and their inabilities, and these beautiful attributes make you human and give your child permission to do the same. We are role models, we are not perfect and we cannot always remain positive. We will have our buttons pushed, we will have our off days, we will question our place, our parenting style and our abilities. And this is just exactly what positive parents do.

Counselling gives the child the ability to see his or her place in the family. This is called family systems theory, this is often not a conscious thing, this is the strength of the Sandplay, it allows the wounded child ego to resolve any issues of which are acted out in things like bed wetting or tantrums. Although the list is long, as individuals we experience our own family differently, this is seen in the different coping mechanisms put in place by the wounded child ego, you may have a quiet child who you think is just shy or introverted, the Sandtray may reveal a different side. Not forgetting there are emotions connected to the issues such as;

anger, resentment, fear which are also attached to a belief. Working on the issues also helps to bring up the emotions and it is at this point the ego self uses the unconscious to restore the new found beliefs.

As the child develops values of others, which are not akin to the essence of the personality of the child, tiny seeds are planted in the form of words and actions, words are powerful such as; *you are a stupid girl, you never shut up, you don't need brains you have looks,* etc. These values and beliefs placed on the child throughout their development stages can be damaging. It is important to note here that children differ greatly, some are more sensitive than others, and these sensitive children will harbour more resentment.

As parents it is best to not get caught up in thinking we are responsible for every moment, or memory in a child's life. This is simply not the case, a good parent is an authentic parent and if this means you showing all aspects of your personality and feel comfortable with this, then you are being true to yourself and your values. This is how children learn good values; a child playing up may be testing boundaries, transitioning to another stage or simply unhappy with a change in the family dynamic.

The more parents foster positive values, the stronger the neural pathway and as a result the child will learn to use this thinking as their default. If any stage of development is not met fully, the child will not have a positive default and will retain a negative pattern of thinking that will repeat itself through every stage in the life cycle from childhood to adolescence and adulthood. This can explain why some teenagers are still acting like young kids, because when an issue arises they react, they go back to a childhood stage and age of development.

The main aim of Sandplay is to restore a healthy ego balance back to the child. In order to do this a new or positively re-enforced way of thinking needs to be instilled, this translates to building new neural pathways in the mind. The more the positive thought is re-enforced, the stronger the pathway. In this way he or she can tap into their own unique personalities and find pleasure in living an authentic life.

Children inherit their parent's beliefs, the seeds may lie within them dormant, in wait of nurturing, the seed lies just below the surface in the subconscious, waiting to be nurtured. 50% of a child's makeup is filled with the essence of parents, carried on through the line of the mother or father, inherited beliefs are simply that, inherited. These beliefs passed on by adults sit at the surface waiting to control thoughts and behaviours; these are felt as invisible forces.

A parent's beliefs are usually aligned to a certain mindset, fixed mindsets will see parents holding on to old values, old beliefs. A growth mindset will see parents as open minded and easily transition their thinking towards learning and change. Using the many guides available such as Erikson's Psychosocial stages, Neumann's ego development, you can assess the child's seat of developmental processing, this will allow you to further see issues such as mistrust, guilt or shame, of which you can then gently weave into the conversation. The role the parent plays in the Child's development and wellbeing is considerable.

The ability to observe people and their surroundings, listen to their stories in a non-judgmental way is the best gift of connecting in an emphatic manner using the principles of here and now. As the parent, this allows the connection to be viewed through various lenses and techniques that have progressed from the day the child was born through the stages of childhood.

Parenting is much like the therapeutic process where 'attending' is a way that brings out your curiosity, whilst thinking about the existential aspect and questions such as where does my child belong? What is my purpose in their life? This allows your own psyche to open up to innumerable equations, the questions take you on a self-reflecting journey into your past and present, they lead you to more questioning, which takes you into realms of your own self exploration, into links with ancient ancestors, your relationship with God, Goddess, the unconscious collective.

Travelling to this deeper realm allows you to remember the conception, the gestation, the birth, the growth and rekindles the mother-child bond. Even if the bond in your memory was tainted with negative emotions, now is the time to replant seeds of the positive times, the achievements and the moments of true bliss shared with your child. Remember you are also creating new neural pathways. This is the extent to which you need to be prepared to travel and in so doing you honour the space being held between your child and yourself.

Qualities to possess in which will help develop your abilities to guide your child are quiet contemplation, your own therapy processes, hobbies for reflection purposes, exercise for movement, writing, knowledge gathering, Mindfulness meditation and other best self-qualities that you possess in your own self-equation – an open mind is key here.

Positive psychology introduces us to the character traits, to our strengths, behaviours and weaknesses, it includes emotional intelligence. Its roots lie in the REBT model. We have been given a smorgasbord of character traits to choose from at will. All these traits, give us our unique personalities, and free will, determines what you do with what you have been given.

For example, you were told by your parents, who were great people but very old fashioned in their thinking that "girls can't be CEO's". When that dream position comes up, the one you have always secretly or not so secretly wanted, you hesitate on the offer. Why? You still carry your parent's beliefs, its deep but it is there. Sandplay will bring it to the surface and positive psychology, Mindfulness and other techniques can show you, that yes, you do have the strengths of leadership, humanity, communication and authenticity. What better attributes for a CEO, go for it.

There is substantial research into how social support during stressful and difficult times is essential for resilience and wellbeing. Recently, researchers asked a different question, that of the role of social support, and the role social support plays during good times and the impacts on wellbeing and relationships. One of the main findings was that sharing good news contributed to wellbeing, this in fact was above and beyond the impact of the good event itself. This effect *'capitalising'*; being able to relive a wonderful experience all over again by telling the story creates positive energy, which serves to energise us and instils positive emotions beneficial for good health and wellbeing.

The good news story takes on a unique language and the language here has a positive connotation which vibrates at a certain frequency and this is a feel good note. In my practice and workshops, I often ask clients to write a 'letter of gratitude', for this very reason. As the law of attraction would have it if you feel good you attract others with the same energy. We know from research that certain frequencies resonate at a vibration level that takes on a healing frequency. Resonating positivity and being the bearer of good news creates the formation of the ripple effect!

Parents and children possess many different types of character strengths including skills, talents, interests or intellectual emotions; however, these strengths do not necessarily reflect the real you or who you are that you feel you are, your inner being. Understanding your character strengths and those of your children, opens up the possibilities to knowing just how capable individuals really are when placed in diverse situations. Character strengths are the personality traits that make you authentic, strong and resilient. Personality can either hide in your unconscious mind or emerge in consciousness. This is part of the process in self-development, discovering parts of yourself within your self-equation.

Knowing that your subconscious or unconscious shapes your reality especially the programming from birth to 6 years, it is important to ascertain the difference between your conscious thoughts and a programmed thought. Most of the time we are in default to the subconscious, which means we function on automatic pilot using the patterns conditioning learnt from childhood and are consciously thinking, that is the here and now moment only a small amount of time. The majority of the time we sit in the unconscious mind, your conditioning shapes your reality. Knowing this fact, it makes it even more important to have good memories on which to draw on, and having developed good stages in the life cycle will enhance this experience. If your thinking is that of a victim or sabotage mentality, it is possible to change this belief.

By changing your programming in your unconscious mind through de-programming or conditioning to a positive default thinking style using self-love, gratitude or compassion, all of which operate in the here and now, you can enjoy a positive relationship with yourself, which opens up your energy to attract positive relationships with others, the law of attraction 101. This is the area I focus on in my workshops and retreats using Mindfulness. Knowing your strengths can allow you to move towards a positive mindset. This area is a part of the results of intense training in Mindfulness which can deliver a great result, turn a life around and allow individuals of all ages to flourish.

Fiona Werle

# *The Mother Child Synergy of Bonding*

*Everybody has chosen their own path. There is no right or wrong. Some have come down in groups to share a collective experience. It doesn't mean we have to be complacent. We are all in this together. Wisdom is knowledge, knowledge is power. Acceptance leads to self-growth*

The mother child bond connection is an important one, it starts in the womb where both mother and child will share a synchronised heart rate, this synchronicity is part of the bonding and creates a chemical reaction where oxytocin is released, and this is the love hormone. If this is the beginning to a new life, then the result can only be that of a flourishing family. Unfortunately, life can sometimes get in the way and there comes a need for an intervention. Recognising the need is a sign of good parenting; it instils a growth mindset in the child and allows them to build resilience around connections.

It is important to remember here that there should be no judgment made on a mother as a result of disconnection with her child. Every parent comes with their own self-equation and as each and every generation develops according to their parent's beliefs and the environment, awareness levels will differ. A disconnect can occur as a result of difficulties experienced in child

35

birth, post-natal depression, grief or loss. Becoming a parent for the first time is the biggest life challenge you will ever experience.

A dis-connect could occur because a mother has returned to full time work, having another baby, divorce, death, change of country and the list goes on. Sometimes a sensitive child may, as a result of change experience physical illness or discomfort such as colic, the change may present as fearsome obstacles to the child's sense of comfort and safety. Safety is a basic need, once the child perceives that this is taken away from them a child can experience depression.

Remember the balance here and see that this is a normal state of depression, attachment loss then reattaching. Mother nature is priming the baby for further self-development and this will require the ability to become resilient around relationships, of coping with being apart from mother.

Remember a young baby cannot verbalise their discomfort, so it becomes an emotion held in their body. Safety is the basic need required for normal development as set out in Maslow's Hierarchy of Needs. Because the baby does not yet have an experience of its body as separate from the mother, the baby experiences these disturbances as the loss of the mother, this is how a memory of trauma, stress or anxiety is induced.

The crucial factor here is the mother as the archetype in the child's psychic development. The self defence mechanism in the baby/child could manifest as aggression, anger, guilt, or grief to what has been lost. In the case of a baby with colic, it could be pent up anger – released!

As a baby, Sue's biological mother knew she was to be adopted, at 16 she was unable to care for her baby. Upon birth, Sue was taken from her birth mother, washed, swaddled and taken to the nursery. She was given the basic needs, fed and cared for by whoever was on duty in the maternity ward, until at three to four weeks old her adoptive parents came and collected her. Sue said that in her new home she had colic and screamed for the first three weeks. This psychosomatic reaction is the baby's process of showing anger, frustration, hurt and fear. The early biological mother child bonding had been disconnected. Her basic needs of food and shelter were met however, the sense of safety was absent and this can lead to later issues of trust. Sue said her adopted mother looked after her just as if she was her own flesh and blood. Sue now realises there was a need to recognise this short period of time in her early life and to relive the anger she felt towards her birth mum for abandoning her.

In reliving the pain, she was able to release it from her body. This was done using the Sandtray and role playing with the therapist, using language as a tool to unleashing symbols we were able to role play and she could ask, "why did you leave me, I was all alone, I was frightened and scared", she released the memory of the trauma from her body, mind and soul and in so doing, changed her self-equation, breaking patterns, and changing old beliefs.

How the therapist works around this will be entirely up to the individual, some may use their own personal skills; others will be trained in Gestalt, NLP, and counselling, coaching, or other therapies. There is no right or wrong, the aim is to get the adult to recognise this early childhood trauma and to release the memory. This is where we are allowing the client to use the brain plasticity which in turn leads to choice in life's new direction; movements in the self-equation.

One thing to remember is, it is never too late to repair the mother child bond connection. If you as a parent are feeling disconnected towards your own mother, then you are carrying this energy within you and your child will be picking up on the subtle messages in the form of energy that you are resonating. There was a reason for the original disconnect, it served at the time, but it does not serve you now. To heal your child may mean to heal your own wounds. Unfortunately there are some cases where the bonding on a psychical and emotional level is hindered, this is usually because of a mental illness, it is best to concentrate on a spiritual bonding in these cases.

One method of rekindling a disconnected Mother Child bond, as an adult is to write a letter of gratitude. We think too much about what goes wrong and not enough about what goes right in our lives. Of course bad events happen and we need these to grow and learn. We tend to think more about these bad events than is helpful. Worse still is that focusing on the negative sets us up for anxiety and depression. One way to keep this from happening is to get better at thinking about and savouring what went well in our life, and the people that were a part of that.

We are all very good at dwelling on the bad, we are wired for fight, flight or freeze, however we are living in a new age whereby there is no need for our minds to dwell in the negative, now is time to allow forward growth and development. This increases our health and wellbeing both psychically and psychologically.

Working on and practicing the skill of 'what went well' can be done by writing a letter of gratitude. Gratitude can make your life happier and more satisfying. When we feel gratitude we benefit from pleasant memories of a positive event in our life. Also when we express gratitude, in the form of a gratitude letter to others, we strengthen our relationship with them.

If you have a parent or sibling that is still living and you would like to bring back the bonds, then write them a letter, talk about the good times, remember what they did for you, no matter how small. Hold on to this memory, send them the letter and revel in the pleasant sensation this small gift has brought you and them. Often this may be an impossible task for whatever reason, the important thing to remember is that this is your self-development and each and every generation will benefit if you as mother can retain a bond with your child. Perhaps all is required is unconditional acceptance, self-acceptance or acceptance of your life's situation.

The crystal is pushed down into the sand, this woman was adopted, and no one is looking at the centre crystal, which represents the new-born baby and the dis-connected mother child bond.

# How Mythology and Fairy-tale Plays into Our Deep Psyche

*Such a small portion of infinite and immeasurable time is allotted to each of us. It is so quickly swallowed up by eternity. How small is the clod of earth on which you crawl. Remember all these things and consider nothing great but this; do what nature bids you, and suffer what Life brings.*

*Marcus Aurelius*

Our race, the human race is extremely old; we have a history that dates back to the Sumerians and Mesopotamians before Egypt. It is from these times that our archetypes formed and our collective consciousness holds the memory of these ancient forefathers/mothers. Our world today is a reflection of our world gone by. Both worlds, our modern and ancient world overlap as a consequence of the great time line that is the forever bond between humans. This bond keeps our collective memory alive; for Eastern cultural beliefs it serves as the bondage of karma and sends our souls to complete its journey.

History is written by the victor, so it is important when we think of Mythology and Fairy-tale, that we see therein lies many a great stories whose beginnings were formed from a place in time. When we think of angels as messengers of God, as imaginary winged creatures, can we be open to the idea that these 'winged creatures' could be an actual part of history, that dragons existed as winged creatures written into the ancient texts and drawings of the Sumerian culture and that in fact they are not myths.

## Mythology

Records exist to say that the Earth was inhabited some 432,000 years ago. Our history of who we are and where we came from has many aspects to it, and the clues can be found in ancient text and mythology. Our very own cells hold our memories; our memories remind us of our place in times gone by; without memory there is no past.

Have you ever been to a place, town or country and just had the sense that you had been there before? I once had an experience whilst travelling through Scotland. I had hired a car and made the decision to take the high road, just like in the song. As I drove this road it felt like I was on automatic pilot, I instinctively knew the curves of the road, I sensed the hidden driveways and I felt so completely at home driving this part of the Scottish highland. It was my first time in Scotland. I went on to have many experiences in this country that made no sense at all.

Each culture has its own unique creation myth and so from here we find ourselves today still asking that question of who am I and where do I come from? This existential question pondered over the centuries by scholars and laymen, children and adults alike. This age old question can be explored through Sandplay, here we can determine our archetypes, the symbols that we choose and get a glimpse into our deepest inner self. I often hear adults say of a piece 'this reminds me of my grandmother, she had it sitting on her shelf'.

Freud used the metaphor of an iceberg to describe the two major aspects of human personality. As you can see in the image, the conscious mind is just the 'tip of the iceberg', beneath the water is the much larger bulk of the iceberg which represents the unconscious. Freud believed a vital part of the mind was the unconscious where things are hidden from awareness, and exerted the greatest influence over our personalities and behaviours. Here resides the collective unconscious as spoken of by Carl Jung. It is within the collective unconscious that the archetypes reside, but here also resides the complexes. Images for children are used in the sand tray to make sense of these complexes. For example is a child has a disconnect with mother, then he or she may have a mother complex. The images used in the sand tray represent for that child the emotion that best represents this complex, whether it be a feline, a tiger, an elephant or even a shoe, the image holds the meaning.

Nurturing Mother

**Fairy-tale**

Snow, as in Snow White and the Seven Dwarfs and other fairy-tale were written by the brothers Grimm, Jacob and Wilhelm. Jacob was a German philologist, jurist and mythologist. The original fairy-tale were first published in 1812 and were steeped in shadow, such as the wicked step mother, a pregnant but innocent Rapunzel, Mother Hilde as supreme Goddess disguised as an old crone.

The depths at which Jacob Grimm translated his figures through mythology and folklore were taken from even earlier stories of which many other versions exist throughout Europe. The symbolism is different; such as the magic mirror which is a dialogue with the Goddess moon in an Armenian version. An ancient version dated back to 1750 AD, has the evil stepmother asking her beautiful parrot "who is more beautiful, I or Padmarati?" In some versions knights replace dwarfs and snow white herself is a warrior princess.

As you can see, where you originate from, or even where one or both of your parents or grandparents were from in the world, will determine in early childhood which symbols are introduced into your life and these will come to represent certain emotions. Snow White may bring up a childhood memory of good times, fun times, laughter etc., or for some children they may be tormented by the idea that Snow White is being hunted down by the wicked witch and this is enough to scare some infants. How a child has been parented will determine how well or not they deal with the images, meaning the emotions triggered around an image, its meaning.

A modern version on the importance of archetypes can be found in the movie 'Rise of the Guardians'. Jack Frost is invisible and he just wants to be seen by the children, he is asking himself the existential questions of who am I? What is my purpose? Where did I come from? Where is my meaning? The Easter Bunny, Tooth Fairy, Father Christmas and the Sandman are confronted with their own dilemmas and questions of faith, belief and life's purpose. The boogey man puts the fear into the children and the overwhelming power of fear spreads through the collective consciousness of the children of the world. This is the concept as set out by Carl Jung where he believed that, the universal mythic characters and archetypes reside within the collective unconscious of all people.

Themes are surrounded in personal development, the story has a beginning a middle and an end, and the moral to the story is, how can I have my voice heard, how can I make people look at me, hear me, accept me, for who I am. For the other characters they are questioning their own faith within themselves, self-doubt and self-worth are themes attached to this stage. The overriding sense covers the age old existential question, Who Am I? What is my Purpose in Life?

Each child creates their story in the sand using images. The tip of the ice-berg is what the child shows to the world, underneath lies their inner deeper self, unconscious mind, the further down the deeper the emotion. Children store these emotions in their memories, the Sandtray uncovers them using the images, symbols characters as archetypes in the fairytale pictures that we as parents read to them, or they see on television or in the cinema. The words the parents use reinforce messages which builds the memory, for example; Snow White was a good girl, just like you, or that wicked witch reminds me of your big sister. These words associated with the fairytale symbols become the memory of the child and add to their vocabulary.

*Characters in the original book by William Joyce – Guardians of Childhood. We see these images as archetypes.*

Fiona Werle

# Learn how Eastern Philosophy Influences our Thinking Today

---

*In the heavens, water takes the form of clouds. Once the clouds rise, it will not be long before rain falls. Even as rain rises to the heavens, it is preparing to fall – whereby all life is nourished and refreshed.*

*I Ching*

---

In Eastern philosophy they have the Yin and Yang. Yang is a representation of the active, warming, upward movement, day and summer. Yin is the still, cool, resting, night, winter and solid. Within the yin yang equation are the elements of fire, water, wood, metal and earth. These symbols are used in Eastern Astrology and the I Ching (Book of Changes). Astrology and travel directions are represented by twelve earthly branches found in the Heavens, these symbols of animals are: horse, sheep, monkey, rooster, dog, pig, rat, ox, tiger, rabbit, dragon and snake, representing stages of growth and death.

Heaven represents the invisible, vibrational world where

earth is visible, dense and solid. These basic principles are the foundations of the philosophy of Feng Shui. Here we see clearly the archetypes and symbols that the Eastern people have inherited in their collective unconscious.

Sacred Geometry is the alignment of heaven to earth, the invisible powers of the lines of the meridians, or the energy lines that can be found in and around our earth grid and our bodies, known as chakras. We can calculate the complexities of energy points of the human bodies which have been around for thousands of years in the form of acupuncture, acupressure and other healing forms.

The ancient cultures knew this information and spoke of it in folklore, tradition, dreamtime and in medicine, such as advanced acupuncture which dates back thousands of years. The idea that some ancient tattoos have a therapeutic purpose has been suggested before. For example, 5300-year-old Ötzi the Iceman, the oldest European mummy, was tattooed with acupuncture lines and crosses on his back and legs.

Some Eastern philosophy has been driven over to the west, through modern media, tourism and immigration. Westerners have taken to this philosophy with a sense of openness and embraced the symbol of the Yin and Yang, Feng Shui, meditation and Yoga. German missionary Richard Wilhelm was the first to translate the I Ching in the 19th century, and Carl Jung recognised the symbols as representing the theory of synchronicity of the unconscious. This area then becomes the ground on which self-development is based and indeed within this teaching Sandplay finds shared principles.

If you are unfamiliar with the I Ching or Book of Changes it is a very in-depth book that incorporates the Chinese astrology, Feng Shui and other elements. It serves as a book of divination, a guide to life, a type of olden time self-help book.

Yin and Yang are the representatives of the universe before time memorial; it means ultimate nothingness, the symbol for the birth, creation of all fundamental laws. The polar opposites, black and white, duality, the circle, male, female, receptive, active, warming, cooling, light, dark, sun, moon, birth, death. This symbol is the continuous cycle of life, with one unable to exist without the other. Profound as a symbol, simplistic in design, yet whether you are of Eastern or Western origin this symbol speaks to a part of our psyche.

Many of our modern systems of psychology have been founded on the philosophies of Eastern approaches to health and wellness.

Yin Yang image with the I Ching lines of change

# Uncover the Importance of Anthropology and Archetypes

*We are all a sum of our parts, our self-equation is made up of our ancient ancestor's beliefs, our modern day beliefs and our shared beliefs. Finding the balance of where we sit on the Polarity of Balance must include all our parts to make us feel fully whole.*

Anthropology is the discipline of humanities, social and natural sciences and their relationship with one another. Anthropology builds upon knowledge from natural sciences, including the discoveries about the origin and evolution of early humans, our ancestors, human physical traits, behaviour, and the differences and how the evolutionary past of early civilisation has influenced the organisation of human social and cultural relations, institutions, and social conflicts. Early anthropology has been central in the development of several interdisciplinary fields such as cognitive science, global studies, and various ethnic studies including ecopsychology.

Ecopsychology is our psyches relationship with the natural environment, sacred sites, churches, temples, sacred buildings, mountains, springs and other places, connections through Mindfulness, nature, prayer or ritual are known as ecotherapy. Some people hug trees, this is not simply being a 'greeny' this is connecting to a natural source, feeling the soothing invisible patterns of nature and the pure natural environment. Gardeners and farmers often have a unique connection with the natural environment, using their knowledge of the seasons, the moon phases to know when to sow and when to reap.

Our ancestors, the traditional and archaic people saw the world in animistic terms, think of the Pagan tradition, the harvest was a time of coming together as community and celebrating abundance. Our deep rooted collective unconscious is in touch with ecological intelligence, the seasons and the numerous changes they bring with them.

Jung stated that there must be some connection between related events, he called this the ecological principle; *where everything is a part of everything else, such as the human mind is connected to and in tune with and between things and event, leading to the ability to see and sense in another way.* He described these events and the relationship between them as synchronicity.

Synchronicity in quantum physics can be seen as a morphic field; this realm includes telepathy (when the mother knows the exact moment when the baby has woken up), intuition, memory, and the collective consciousness. *Morphic resonance is a process whereby self-organising systems inherit a memory from previous similar systems. In its most general formulation, morphic resonance means that the so-called laws of nature are more like habits. The hypothesis of morphic resonance also leads to a radically new interpretation of memory storage in the brain and of biological inheritance*

This invisible realm is another place where we can find some sense of purpose and meaning, here we can see that the polar opposites, duality and shadow personality are all a fundamental part of our collective inheritance. The attraction of opposites and their interplay opens up our awareness, leading to a deeper understanding that our lives are connected through synchronicity or morphic resonance.

Ancient sites, ceremonial landscapes (Stone Henge, Delphi, Temple Mount, Pyramids, Women's caves etc.) still hold an archaic whisper or morphic resonance, still heard by some. The Australian Aboriginals, Native American Indians, South American Natives still have a strong connection with the land. Our landscapes are covered in multiple layers of symbols; ancient architecture used precise measurements known by the masters of sacred geometry to build such buildings as the pyramids, churches, steeples, castles etc. and our natural monuments stand in our traditional archaic memory. Uluru is sacred to indigenous Australians and believed to be about 700 million years old.

Our churches too, hold a unique spiritual energy, with buildings such as the Pantheon in Rome, Italy, Pantheon meaning, "every god". This building gives a calm sense of being held, and when one looks up at the fresco ceiling we see, represented, all the gods of each culture and religion; Paganism, Judaism, Hinduism, Christianity and Islam, the huge dome gives a sense of being in the womb, in fact this ancient church is dedicated to St Mary.

Manmade mounds and pyramids found all over the world are just some of the other buildings; some used as burial sites others housed great leaders above, in the temples. Places on earth that are sacred sites, vortexes, cosmological centres that reflect as above, so below all an integral part of our ancient psyche. In many parts of Europe, we find healing water springs, and our oceans are driven by the moons invisible force to create the ebb and flow of the great oceans tides.

The Pyrenean Mountain region known as Catalonia has been home to a race of peoples whose antiquity embraces stories of 'faeries', mermaids, dragons and bears. An area steeped in diverse cultural changes and traditions with a fusion of ancient

Paganism, Judaism, Christianity and Islam. Many of the traditions are steeped in the rituals of the ancients' beliefs connected to woodland forces, fire and fertility, farming and death. The fairy-tale, legends and customs hold deep mythical elements stored within the collective unconscious of the people of this area.

Today we have TV shows like Game of Thrones that incorporate archetypes, such as Heroin, Ruler, Elder, Guardian, Hunter/Predator, Martyr, Sycophant, Temptress, Thief, Victim and Warrior. The game industry has tapped into the power of archetypes to develop an industry of millions of gamers who have formed communities around games such as Skyrim – The Elder Scrolls. This game is wrought with ancient archetypes, dragons, castles, magicians, alchemy, weapons, metallurgy, fighting, ancient scrolls and books, which keeps the audience traveling through this ancient world in search of clues which will eventually lead them to The Elder Scrolls.

# *How we Discover Symbols and Archetypes*

---

*Biological inheritance need not all be coded in the genes, or in epigenetic modifications of the genes; much of it depends on morphic resonance from previous members of the species. Thus each individual inherits a collective memory from past members of the species, and also contributes to the collective memory, affecting other members of the species in the future. B. Lipton*

---

Images are the symbols and archetypes, we have recognised that symbols and archetypes are integrated into our psyche through the process of stored memory which can be carried through the morphic field, a universe with its own inherent memory, if you are a Dr Who fan this is how he travels in his Tardis, along the morphic field full of memory from every living soul.

Are we still discovering new symbols, are some archetypes in our field of vision, yet our awareness has not processed them as a part of our meaning and purpose in life. Looking up we have the sky, the stars and the Heavens, where our forefathers/mothers (and some remaining cultures) sailed the seas using only the celestial night sky as their map. These star readers wrote the language of animals into the sky, giving us heavenly archetypes such as; Sagittarius, the Warrior with his bow and arrow, Leo the proud Lion, Gemini the twins, Scorpio, Aries, Aquarius, Capricorn, Libra Virgo, Cancer, Taurus and Pisces. The division of the ecliptic into the signs of the zodiac originated in Babylonian (Chaldean) astronomy during the first half of the 1st millennium BC. Each sign represents a period of time, a season bringing forth new growth, harvest and dormancy; each generation adopts their own unique symbols of birth, growth and death. Death as we will explore in another chapter is an area in Western culture that we lack understanding and awareness around. Another ancient symbol that captures this theme of life and death, is that of the Ouroboros.

The Ouroboros is an ancient symbol depicting a serpent or dragon eating its own tail. It symbolises self-reflexivity or the cycles of constantly re-creating itself. The phoenix as seen in the film Harry Potter, is another example of birth and re-birth. The Ouroboros and the phoenix represent the idea of primordial unity related to something existing from the beginning with such force it cannot be extinguished.

While first emerging in Ancient Egypt and India, the Ouroboros has been important in religious and mythological symbolism, but it has also been frequently used in alchemical illustrations, where it symbolises the circular nature of the alchemist's opus. This alchemical process has been referred to symbolically as the substance of the philosopher's stone and is associated with the Elixir, Holy Grail, Eternal Life, Divinity, Quintessence and the Christ. It is also often associated with Gnosticism, Hermeticism and Hinduism.

Carl Jung interpreted the Ouroboros as having an archetypal significance to the human. The makers of the film, Lord of the Rings had another interpretation in mind, that of eternal searching, a quest and the struggles associated with each individual's journey to find their true purpose and meaning in life.

The Sun and the Moon are the polar opposites, the sun represents heat and day, the moon cooling at night, sun the conscious mind and the moon the unconscious; the interaction of these two luminaries highlights our psychological movements, our persona represented by the sun energy shows a side of our personality to the world that is shallow, guarded, very different to that of our moon energy which represents our deep emotions.

*Ouroboros, a representation of the cycle birth, growth and death*

When a child is playing they become their heroes, heroines, villains or princesses. They are tapping into the archetypal characters which allows them to fully express their emotions in play. If you have a child who find it difficult to verbalise their emotions encourage 'dress up', play. Sandplay is another great way for them to express emotions.

The more a child is exposed to images in the form of story books, films and other forms, the more chance a child has in tapping into their chosen archetype or image in the form a character to use as an expressive form of non-verbal communication.

Fiona Werle

# *Dream Interpretation and Your Child*

---

*Is all that we see or seem but a dream within
a dream*

---

Dreams often come to us in the form of metaphor and symbols, sometimes these dreams can be very scary experiences and children will often come to us saying they had a nightmare. We all dream, some of us remember our dreams in great details, others only recall fragments. What is represented in our dreams? Looking at dreams with our logical mind they often do not make sense, a mishmash of symbols or illogical sequence of events.

However, dream interpretation realistically can only be fully interpreted by the dreamer themselves or by someone close to them such as a mother, or another who could understand the symbols or metaphor chosen by the unconscious mind to represent the meaning behind the dream because they are in tune with the dreamer.

A dream can represent an issue that the ego has pushed down into the realm of the unconscious, only for it to arise in the form of a dream. A dream is the mind's way of processing an issue needing to be seen and resolved before it is pushed further down into the depths of the unconscious.

55

Dreams therefore contain the subliminal messaging of symbols collected by our complex human psyche, translated in the dream state. Symbols, personalised, represent the actions or inactions, feelings, beliefs or perceptions of our conscious mind towards an event or issue, presented in symbol form or metaphor. The conscious mind for some reason has pushed these thoughts down into the unconscious realm, perhaps to keep the conscious mind structured. This pushed down content reveals itself back in a dream.

Symbols seemingly scrambled together in our dreams, can at first appear non-sense. However, if we understand that our own life-equation is made up of Self, family, environment, soul and ancestors then we can get a glimpse into dream interpretation. All that we have inherited, seen, heard or felt has a symbol and subliminal messages attached. Just like a fairy-tale is full of the symbols for good, bad, evil and shadow, each symbol represents a memory which we store in our deep psyche.

Dreams are as individual as our own unique life experiences. Each and every concept in our mind has a psychic association, from numbers, letters (old and new), the Runes would resonate with Northern Europeans, the Sumerian cuneiform, Egyptian hieroglyphs to modern day alphabets made available through archaeological digs and movies like Cleopatra have made their way into the western psyche.

In dream interpretation, metaphor is a great tool, alongside the symbols. Jung suggests that it is the primitive mind working with the unconscious to send up these visions that often include animals, plants, stones, and monsters. The symbols of your dreams will align to your own cultural and familial environment.

The role of the dream interpreter is also important in knowing whether there is a need to analyse and delve deeper into why the dream was dreamt, or whether it was enough for the child or adult to have simply processed through dreaming. Much like that of a child in a Sandplay, it is often not necessary to analyse the symbols in the Sandtray, often allowing the child to process their unconscious issues through play is enough.

It is of vital importance to instill good sleeping patterns into your child's daily routine, this has many health benefits and it will train them to be good sleepers in adolescents when sleep is imperative. The natural reflexes of yawning act as a natural stimulant to the vagas nerve which is a natural anti-depressant, so always encourage yawns and sighs, use them as cues that it is a good healthy time for the child to sleep or cat nap.

If you have a teenager and they are staying up late gaming and you are worried about their natural rhythms and health, there is an alternative to having this become a stress related issue, there are orange coloured glasses available which turn the screen orange which reduces the light at night and aids in the circadian rhythm. It is not ideal, but a small solution.

Nocturnal sleep is important and dreams hold a significant place within the control of emotional states and ability to work through emotional issues in the stage 4 deep sleep REM. Sleep is an area of health and wellness that is worth doing your own research into as it has significant impacts on daily functioning. When we think about how a mother supports her new baby through his or her early weeks, months by 3 hourly feeding, it opens up a conversation around mothers ability to cope with this break in their sleep rhythms.

It is not just teenagers and toddlers who need to sleep, we all do. Sleep is a fundamental basic need for our ability to maintain positive mental functioning. A child growing will develop their own patterning of sleep, watch this pattern closely and as a parent look at the signs when your child is ready for sleep.

It is always a good practice to bath a child at night, after diner if possible, dress them in pajamas' , allow them to play in their room and then either snuggle up in bed with them or sit quietly with them to read a book. Instilling rituals such as this enables both parents, carers and the children to know and understand that there is order, boundaries and positive rules governing bed time. But more importantly it keeps the mother/father child bonding strong and gives children a positive experience of shared love and strengthening family bonds.

It is also important to remember that the default mode network functions through reflection, memory and daydreaming. So next time you see your child day dreaming let them be, they are actually raising their brain waves, in a Beta state, a place of no focus, no concern, simply being.

# The Crystal as a Symbol of Our Organic Self

*"farthest removed from the emotions,
feelings, fantasies and things of ego-
consciousness, the stone symbolises the
simplest, deepest experience of something
eternal, giving rise to feeling of immortality
and the unalterable".* C. Jung

A stone or crystal can represent Self on the deepest organic level in the Sandtray. The chemical compounds, elements and minerals that make up the stone or crystal are shared by our own chemical structure; bringing a resonance of synchronicity and knowing as this piece representing our true core self. This symbol represents the inner core of human existence at its most basic level.

Standing between two worlds, Sandplay acts as a bridge to unite the worlds of duality, internal and external, rational and irrational, visible and invisible, conscious and unconscious. The unconscious Self, chooses the images that represent the symbols, which hold the dual meanings formed by the unconscious in early childhood memories.

It is the recognition of images as symbols on a deep psychological level which enables us to cross the bridge to awareness whereby views and perspectives are remolded in accordance with the active forces of the conscious mind; this is the therapeutic advantage, where the conscious connections lead to awareness. This is the process of understanding the complexes, once the child understands that they don't always have to be the 'good' child, then they release this complex.

We can use the example of our young boy who at the vital stage of toilet training, had his needs unmet, therefore his developmental stage i.e. successful toilet training was unsuccessful as a result of his parents fighting. This boy has a need to be the 'good boy', his complex is indeed complex. He holds in his faeces in the need to have a sense of control. If the children during this stage can overcome the conflict it will result in a sense of accomplishment and independence.

*The circle in centre, inside of this a mother cat with her babies, crystals representing ages 1-4. This child at 8, is still finding meaning in the mother child bonding synergy.*

The circle represents wholeness; our inner order containing our true personalities. The circle can appear in the Sandtray surrounding pieces as a boundary, as a drawing in the sand or as symbol for the self. We are always looking at the mother-child relationship. The circle is the womb that holds the unborn baby, the universe that holds the soul, the intellect and collective memory. The circle signifies heaven as a symbol and points toward the spiritual element of the self-equation.

The circle can be a representative of a mandala, holding the self within the universe. In this way the sand picture takes on a deeper meaning, it joins the visible to the invisible.

# Influencing Child's Development with Music and Mandala's

---

*The centre of the Mandala represents the still point of the turning universe, the earth in the geocentric cosmos and the surrounding square symbolises the path of the sun, moon and planets along the ecliptic*

---

We have seen the influence words can have on our child's development, each word is said using a tone of voice; gratefully, lovingly or aggressively. Every note holds a certain frequency and this translates to a vibration. The first sound on earth according to ancient Eastern philosophy was the OM sound (aom) replicated by Buddhist monks in chants and meditations. Not only are these frequencies energising, but they can revitalise and motivate.

Mozart's music holds this resonance as well. This music as a healing aspect ties in to the morphic resonance we mentioned in another chapter. There is also the throat singers of Mongolia who chant, this tradition dates back thousands of years and is said to be the bridge between Heaven and Earth.

Other music using the 432 hertz frequency have been

dubbed 'healing music', because the body can resonate to a place of balance, bringing healing to the cellular and electromagnetic body, 432hz vibrates on the principals of golden ratio, which is one of two basic principles of Sacred Geometry. Sacred Geometry includes the whole spectrum of patterns, shapes and forms that are part of the make-up of all living things that regularly occur in nature.

A quick look at a rain droplet under the microscope for example will highlight the patterns as geometric symbols. As symbols these shapes and patterns, are interesting to explore, and many Mandala's are representations of these biological patterns. If you have a child who is unproductive, poorly focused, ill, irritated, angry or absent of thought, try playing the 432 hertz music in their surroundings and monitor the differences in behaviour over a few days or weeks. A quick search on YouTube will show that there is a lot of choice for healing music in this category.

A happy and healthy crystal represents the child's true essence, the perfect vibrational frequency, 432 hertz music and a mandala. This is sacred geometry, biology, ecopsychology and the symbols of the Sandtray as expressed in one pattern. I once had a client, a young teenager, that asked me why I didn't have any rough rocks to place in the tray, he commented that the crystals were too precious for him to use. We found him a rock. I noticed that after some weeks he no longer used the rock, but instead used a quartz crystal to represent himself in the sandtray.

The word mandala is taken from the Sanskrit language which can be roughly translated as "circle". But the meaning of mandala is not restricted to a simple shape but represents a more complex meaning. The mandala stands for a cosmic diagram that signifies wholeness and can be seen as a model symbolising the configuration of life. The mandala signifies the relation of man to the infinite world extending beyond our physical and mental plane.

The mandala is used in a Buddhist religious context for purposes of meditation and contemplating on the universe. The concept of mandala seems to have originated long before history started, in ancient India when Rigveda used mandala as a collection of chapters or hymns that were chanted during ceremonies which were very much in vogue during this time.

The thought is that the universe originated from these hymns, the sacred sounds of the hymns which held the code or a genetic pattern of things or living beings (morphic resonance) an essence of things around us which is the universe. The mandala is a way to realise that the whole universe is within us (Anthropology, Eco psychology) and a way to enlightenment and understand reality.

I have included a mandala in this book, however there are many more available online to download and colour in. If you are needing some relaxation time, or just a bit of time-out as a parent and you thought colouring in was for children, then think again. Adult colouring in books are all the rage and for good reason. They help to calm the mind, still the inner chatter and the body receives the signal to relax which has a huge health benefit. Next time the kids sit at the dining table to do some colouring in, join them, why not!

Fiona Werle

**Yin and Yang Mandala Colouring In Picture**

Here is a Mandala for you to colour in, if possible put on some healing 423hertz music for greater effect, as the purpose of this is to be in a state of Mindfulness during the whole experience losing yourself in your creativity. Enjoy!

Fiona Werle

# *Erik Erikson's Psychosocial Stages of the Life Cycle*

---

*No individual, community or country can place their values on another. We are all evolving at a different pace. Ancient knowledge runs through your veins.*

---

The model of Psychosocial Stages shows the close relationship between a child's developmental processes that are intertwined with parents/significant others and their environment. Erikson highlights the position that ego plays in dealing with intra-psychic (internal) conflicts when we see good psychological health in the form of Trust versus Mistrust.

We shall be referring to Erikson's Psychosocial Stages of Development Model throughout this book. It can be used as a guide for all parents in their own and their children's road towards self-growth. As with any guide it is best to seek out the advice of a professional when it comes to your child's mental health.

We had the story of the boy who started wetting the bed as a consequence of his inability to travel successfully from the stages of development. For a better understanding of the child's developmental stages, Erik Erikson's psychosocial stages of development is a guide that will help explain the emotions around behaviour.

# Erikson's Psychosocial Stages of Development

### 0-1YR
#### TRUST V'S MISTRUST
IF SIGNIFICANT OTHERS /PARENTS PROVIDE FOR BASIC NEEDS, PHYSICAL AND
EMOTIONAL, INFANT DEVELOPS A SENSE OF TRUST.
IF BASIC NEEDS ARE NOT MET, MISTRUST IN RELATIONSHIPS OCCURS.

### 1-3YRS
#### AUTONOMY V'S SHAME/DOUBT
DEVELOPING AUTONOMY AT THIS STAGE INVOLVING A SENSE OF SELF-RELIANCE AND
SELF-DOUBT. A TIME FOR EXPLORATION, FOR MAKING MISTAKES, TESTING LIMITS AND
EXPERIMENTING.
IF DEPENDENCY ON PARENTS IS ALLOWED, CHILD'S AUTONOMY IS INHIBITED AND
ABILITY TO DEAL WITH SITUATIONS IS HAMPERED.

### 3-6YRS
#### INITIATIVE V'S GUILT
THE BASIC TASK IS TO ACHIEVE A SENSE OF COMPETENCE AND INITIATIVE, GIVEN
FREEDOM TO SELECT PERSONALLY MEANINGFUL ACTIVITIES, CHILD TENDS TO DEVELOP
A POSITIVE VIEW OF SELF AND FOLLOWS THROUGH WITH ACTIVITIES.
IF THE CHILD IS NOT ALLOWED TO MAKE THEIR OWN DECISIONS, THEY TEND TO
DEVELOP GUILT OVER TAKING INITIATIVE. THEY REFRAIN FROM TAKING AN ACTIVE
STANCE AND ALLOW OTHERS TO CHOOSE FOR THEM.

### 6-12YRS
#### INDUSTRY V'S INFERIORITY
A NEED TO EXPAND UNDERSTANDING OF THE WORLD AND DEVELOP GENDER-ROLE
IDENTITY AND LEARN BASIC LEARNING, TO ENABLE A SENSE OF INDUSTRY WHICH
ENABLES A CHILD TO ATTAIN GOALS AND FOCUS.
FAILURE RESULTS IN A SENSE OF INADEQUACY.

## 12-18YRS
### IDENTITY V'S ROLE CONFUSION

A TIME OF TRANSITION BETWEEN CHILDHOOD AND ADULTHOOD. A TIME FOR TESTING LIMITS, BREAKING DEPENDENT TIES AND ESTABLISHING NEW IDENTITY. MAJOR CONFLICTS CENTRE ON CLARIFICATION OF SELF-IDENTITY, LIFE GOALS AND MEANING. FAILURE TO ACHIEVE A SENSE OF IDENTITY RESULTS IN ROLE CONFUSION.

## 18-35YRS
### INTIMACY V'S ISOLATION

DEVELOPMENTAL TASK AT THIS TIME IS TO FORM INTIMATE RELATIONSHIPS. FAILURE CAN LEAD TO ALIENATION AND ISOLATION.

## 35-60YRS
### GENERATIVITY V'S STAGNATION

THERE IS A NEED TO GO BEYOND SELF AND FAMILY AND BE INVOLVED IN HELPING THE NEXT GENERATION. THIS IS A TIME OF ADJUSTING TO THE DISCREPANCY BETWEEN ONE'S DREAM AND ONE'S ACTUAL ACCOMPLISHMENTS. FAILURE TO ACHIEVE A SENSE OF PRODUCTIVITY OFTEN LEADS TO PSYCHOLOGICAL STAGNATION.

## AGE 60+
### INTEGRITY V'S DESPAIR

IF ONE LOOKS BACK ON LIFE WITH FEW REGRETS AND FEELS PERSONALLY WORTHWHILE, EGO INTEGRITY RESULTS.

FAILURE TO ACHIEVE EGO INTEGRITY CAN LEAD TO FEELINGS OF DESPAIR, HOPELESSNESS, GUILT, RESENTMENT AND SELF-REJECTION

# Understanding the Basics of Brain Plasticity

*Originality of knowledge gives a platform for self-discovery, encouraging creativity of thought, authenticity and self-expression.*

The good news is that your brain can change through plasticity, you can achieve this as you go through the processes of letting go old hurts, dysfunctional beliefs that no longer serve you, irrational thoughts that do not serve your higher good and accept that what happened in the past served you then, it does not necessarily serve you now. Your new thinking changes the way you perceive; this is where the new circuitry is created. As a child you adapted and coped.

A child's brain development is forming in stages, as we can see in Erik Erikson's psychosocial stages of development. What we also see is that as adults our developmental stages are also present to 60+. These developmental stages are arenas for learning and growth, each child will present at a stage of their ability or not to develop as part of good healthy psychological childhood wellbeing.

Current research in this field of childhood development has shown that it is possible for a child to experience abnormal childhood development, yet obtain good psychological health and wellness through therapy. Sandplay Technique can allow the child to tap into the developmental stage that was unmet (adults can do this also). It is here that we see the unconscious working towards bringing the mind and body experience into alignment.

Fears, anger, sadness or guilt experienced as a result of childhood development can be met in the Sandtray and resolved through experiencing, acknowledging and accepting the old story and creating a new narrative, image and emotion around it. Children do this through play, working closely with the unconscious, psyche and cellular memory, often words are not necessary as the mind fires up new neurons to set a path for the new beliefs and behaviours instilled through the process of Sandplay.

Through brain plasticity it is possible for children and adults to create a whole new set of values, beliefs and to tap into as yet untouched personality traits, such as courage, curiosity or being centred. Through the process of self-development our true authentic personality traits now have the space to arise and be seen, heard or sensed. This is positive psychology at its best, when you discover your strengths and allow them to take you to parts of self that you had buried deep down.

Through personal development and self-growth, beliefs are replaced, old patterns of thinking are changed and as a consequence, behaviours now match with the new plasticity of the developed brain.

Brain plasticity; *also known as neuroplasticity or cortical remapping, is a term that refers to the brain's ability to change and adapt as a result of experience during infancy and childhood. Modern research has demonstrated that the brain continues to create new neural pathways and alter existing ones in order to adapt to new experiences, learn new information and create new memories.*

When we look at the picture of the neurons in the brain, there appears to be a striking similarity to the roots and branches of a tree. This symbol could be reminiscent of the 'tree of life', giving adage to the fact that our minds are the connection to the visible and invisible life; that we are capable of setting out new shoots of growth.

Human change is a complex process, promoting positive brain plasticity through the entire development stages across the life span is the key to health and wellness. The tools are at hand, they include nurturing self and others, caring, a secure environment and good healthy social structures in place.

*Brain Plasticity, neurons firing up, symbolically this picture looks like a scared geometry pattern.*

Fiona Werle

# *Is Negativity a Characteristic of Child Development*

---

*The stronger and greater your compassion,
the stronger and greater your fearlessness
and confidence. So compassion reveals itself
yet again as your greatest resource and your
greatest protection.*

*The Tibetan Book of Living and Dying*

---

Negativity as a character trait can be a child living in their shadow state, this is a coping mechanism and can lead to a powerful force spiraling downward into a void of darkness and negativity, sucking the very life force from the child's soul. It affects family, friends and the child him or herself emotionally and psychically. Is that seed of negativity just a childhood characteristic or has this negativity, as a symbol, helped them to cope with a childhood experience?

Our default mode as humans is negative, that's just the way Mother Nature primed us. It all ties in with flight, fight, freeze. However, she never meant us to be dark and depressed and lead a life of total negativity or be in our shadow state. Positive psychologists introduced the term positivity ratio. The positivity ratio says our positive to negative emotions when in balance can be measured as approximately 3:1. This means about 3 positive emotions to 1 negative emotion to keep balance in life. This of course is not how to lead your life according to ratios; however, it can be seen as a guide.

When we take a look at what negativity is, our shadow self, we see that a child who has been bullied at school for example, can become the bully later in their schooling, as their way of coping with the experience. The shadow is a persona that inhabits our unconscious and lives in a state of oblivion until our conscious mind becomes aware of the need, in the past, of this shadow as a protector. Multiple personality disorders are shadow and light competing for the spotlight.

What is important to remember is that in order to gain a healthy balance, these shadow sides are best met in the Sandtray and acknowledged for what they are, coping mechanisms, we all need to rely on our inner shadow at times.

This sand picture is from a child who watched her father murder her mother, the child was eight at the time, as can be seen in the number of 8 crystals. When you look closely at the picture you see it is steeped in shadow symbols such as the snarling 3 headed dogs looking directly at the big puppy, the snarling tiger is looking directly at the cute tiger, Grumpy from the 7 dwarfs is looking at Happy, the lady bird is next to the bat, the gentle purple snake is next to the venomous snake in attack mode. The father is represented by the soccer ball and net, and the mother holds the children in embrace. The child of course is very confused and this shadow is a glimpse into a splitting of emotions. Working with the child to see the shadow has allowed her awareness to evolve around her deep held emotions of anger and love. In working this way, we are building resilience and helping her to gain a balanced perspective.

A way of ascertaining a measure or scale can be useful in communicating with children, "how are you today on a scale of 1-10 where 1 is excellent and 10 is I need help", it's a good monitor. In universal terms negativity (shadow) is energy; this energy can be both given and received. You know how sometimes you feel you just don't want to be around a certain person, they repulse you, well that's their energy talking to your energy and like magnets, you are either attracted or repelled. Children can sometimes be lured in if they have not fully developed their resilience.

Energy is an invisible force field that surrounds our bodies, it can be captured in special photo imaging also known as an aura, the aura is also known as Kundalini energy and the Chakra's of our body each have a different colour associated with their energy points. This has been known and taught in Eastern medicine for thousands of years. Each culture has its own interpretation of what negativity is. A person with a high negative energy normally experiences negative emotions such as anger, jealousy or fear; because these emotions are draining, they experience low levels of energy. Wellness is affected when people spend too much time in lower energy states; the Chi, Ki or life-force energy in their bodies might slow down or in certain parts of their body or organs can stagnate. This is the manifestation of an illness, eventually leading to any physical, mental or emotional problems.

This area is where you can look at psychosomatic illness as well, tying it in with having your energy sucked out of you or you putting your energy into a negative area ruminating with negative thoughts and before you know it you have become physically or mentally ill. Children become a part of this cycle with bullying or hanging out with the wrong groups. Parents will experience a change in their child's energy, mood and behaviour as the child experiences the extreme end of the Polarity of Balance.

Negativity is energy; energy can be felt, measured and controlled or healed and channeled elsewhere. Many holistic therapists work on an energetic level and these includes; Naturopaths, Acupuncturist, Reiki, Holistic Counsellors and Kinesiologists, to mention just a few. No matter what method used, staying positive and allowing the balance to come into your child's life isn't such a bad way to live. Lifestyle and wellness is directly connected to the energy you put out and the people you hang out with, of course in the situation of our young girl, she had no control of her circumstances; however, the sand picture served twofold, as a release of emotions and awareness that emotions do lurk in the shadows but don't be afraid of them, look at them, acknowledge them and accept them as part of who you are.

As a parent you may ask, is it time for you to do some spring cleaning in your life? Is it time to seek out purpose and direction, to rein in as much positive vibes into your life that you will allow yourself? I think so, why? As parents we are role models, so our children watch our every step, our patterns become their patterns, our behaviours become their behaviours our beliefs become their beliefs and so on it goes. The greatest gift we can give another is to be the best we can be and allow those around us to be their true authentic selves.

Negativity as a characteristic only becomes a part of our child's development if certain needs are not met. This is obvious when looking at Erik Erikson's stages of development. This guide shows us that if we are seeing signs of negativity or dysfunction, then a simple look at the child's developmental stage can tell you a few things. Firstly, is that the child may be transiting from the one stage to the other and this will bring with it a set of emotions, reactions and resistance; all normal parts of the cycle.

The second sign is that of a child who has not been fully able to transition, here is a perfect opportunity to introduce the Sandplay Technique into their lives, to give them the opportunity to move forward in their development in order to avoid stress and other impacts such as negative anxiety. Sandplay Technique is a wonderful medium in which it allows the child to see that there are positive and negative emotions and finding the balance means feeling all parts of the polarity. In so doing, experiences in their daily lives, school, the playground and home are normalised.

Using this book as a guide, you can tap into other resources such as the Mindfulness techniques, using the music and mandala's. As a parent you do have choice and nobody will know your child quite like you do. Tailor make your own therapy, introduce good habits, like sitting down at the dinner table as often as you can and discuss your day or week as a family unit. This is a great opportunity for other discussion and maybe some bantering, storytelling (dads are good at this," I remember when"...) or even debate. All these skills serve your child in the wider world, good communication skills are essential for healthy living.

The possibilities to encourage your child to smell the roses lies with you, the parent, remember you are the role model, your attitude, words and actions are being closely watched. Perhaps start to be the observer of your own lifestyle, are you happy and content, or do you need to make some changes for yourself? As we have mentioned this is not about blaming anybody, it is as it is. Today however is a great day to implement some shifts, slow and easy wins the race.

Nobody is born negative, it is our environment, family, mother bonding and even our circumstances around our conception which will all determine how we manifest as individual characters and personalities. The family structure is the learning ground for all children, and adults. We can all learn from each other, what a gift.

# How Anxiety Impacts your Child

*It is a general human weakness to allow things uncertain and unknown to set us up in hope or plunge us into fear.*

*Gaius Caesar*

In this 21st century where our senses are bombarded on a daily basis with new information and technology it is not surprising that there is a discussion of stress related anxiety having reached children at a younger age. Early childhood centres are seeing our youngest children with ever increasing levels of anxiety. The question is whether this increase in childhood anxiety lies inside or outside of the child's control.

The human body is an intricate system, functioning to maintain good mental and physical health. When this balance is upset, a chain reaction of sequences occurs which lead to a break-down of functioning, children can be affected mentally or physically. We touched briefly on the child complaining of a sore tummy as a symptom of an upset. An upset in this area is hitting the core of the child's being, and it could relate to a stress brought on by outside factors, such as a parental break-up, disharmony in the house, a new sibling, all manner of situations can be likely to affect a sensitive child.

If you add to this, stress from daily life, school or environment, then it is no wonder we have an epidemic of children suffering from anxiety. Although parents and carers must be very careful with their diagnoses of anxiety, always remembering that there is good and bad anxiety. When I was young it was called nerves and my mother would say 'do you have butterfly's in your tummy", this was good anxiety. Often I felt sick in new situations, this was anxiety, I grew out of this because I learnt to be resilient, however it was never explained that anxiety was a natural state and nothing to be afraid of, certainly when I was young nobody said I would go on to suffer depression as a result of the bad anxiety taking over my younger life. I had no coping skills.

The degree of anxiety encountered can be determined by biological factors, psychological disorders, personality type, social norms and inherited beliefs. We see this on a daily basis in child care centres where children are not joining in with play, or are coming to day-care sick, tired and grumpy. Another aspect to anxiety can be seen in the movements of the self-equation, including 'what's happening between mum and dad', and the home environment. Including Sandplay Technique as an integral part of play in child care centres would serve a great healing role for any child unable to cope or explain their feelings.

Anxiety is a very complicated functioning within the human body and mind connection. The human mind houses the limbic system, containing the hippocampus, amygdala and the hypothalamus the emotional centre of the brain. Our brain determines the direction stress will manifest in the child's development emotionally and behaviourally. Our body talks to us through pain, discomfort and illness, a physical signal could be an upset tummy.

Every aspect of the mind has a body connection; remember we store our memories in our cells. Left to stagnate, these illnesses can lead to chronic health problems so it is important at this point to enable children to develop healthy ego's and we can now do this by allowing the Sandplay to take on that role of enabling further development also teaching our children to 'let go' through Mindfulness, teaches them the body mind connection, so that when they have a pain they are able to make the emotional connection. Talking up their strengths will help to build their resilience.

All emotions are registered in the brain or hypothalamus whether positive or negative to form an electrical charge which creates chemical activity corresponding to that part of the brain which regulates the response mechanisms. *"The amygdala is positioned to intercept sensory information and if deemed a potential threat immediately fire off volleys of impulses that can change our behaviour."*

Albert Ellis founder of Rational Emotive Behavioural Therapy (REBT) believed that the key to unlocking blockages from a person's mind is through changing the self-talk. Self-talk is a response to an external event which triggers automatic negative thought. *"Cognitive Behavioural therapy is based on the assumption that, a reorganisation of one's self-statement will result in a corresponding re-organisation of one's behaviour."* Negative talk or rumination is the repetitive and negative thinking about some event or someone. Often coined the monkey mind, left to its own devices, the mind can be a powerful destructive force.

Positive psychology has shown that Mindfulness is a powerful tool in helping to stop that rumination even in younger children. I have included a Mindfulness meditation in this book for everyone to use. Alternatively, colouring in the mandalas whilst listening to Mozart or 432Hz music will also have a relaxing effect.

The REBT model shows the ABC basics of A=Activating Event, why is my child unhappy. B= Beliefs, I should, I must, catastrophizing, irrational thinking. C=Consequence, anxiety, depression, misbehaving. This model allows parents to use a systemic approach to pin pointing some disruptors and using the holistic approach of role modelling so the child can learn to become more resilient and accepting of all situations. This will help to relieve anxiety and change the Childs focus.

An example of this comes with forgiveness, if a parent is able to forgive say their own parents using the approach of unconditional love, this act serves to bring about awareness, to identify irrational beliefs held around parenting, which opens up the space to dispute these beliefs and in so doing create a new way of thinking around emotions, behaviour. As we have said all along, parents can be the best role models for better or worse. The worst case scenarios are harder to accept, yet with acceptance comes new perspectives, tolerance for others and greater compassion.

Mindfulness relaxation is the key to quieting the monkey mind and stopping the negative thoughts or rumination. The plasticity that comes with Mindfulness acts to re-organise behaviour, build new neural pathways, unlocks blockages, helps to change self-talk or eliminates the monkey mind and in essence we become more in control of our thinking, which limits anxiety. These are all tools of which children and adults can use to gain control or to stay in control of emotional flare-ups. Counting and breathing is a very simple way to begin.

Stress affects a person's health in two ways, according to Ogden and Seward, firstly by causing changes in behaviour and then by producing changes in the body, changes in the nervous system, the endocrine system and the immune system. Diseases that have been linked to these systems include hypertension, rheumatism, arthritis, asthma, diabetes, heart disease and cancer. As we know, these diseases do not differentiate between age and gender.

Another aspect to be mindful of is social connectedness which is beneficial irrespective of whether one is under stress. Generally social support is intended as the *"psychological and material resource provided by others that help one's ability to cope with stress."* Also *"stress hormones erode brain architecture, impair the immune system, burden the heart and weaken resistance to mental disorders such as anxiety and depression."* Maintaining social relationships and offering individuals support is also a way of influencing healthy

81

behaviours. Joining a parenting group, play group or social group is a form of therapy for parents and children and some emotional support through Sandplay and Mindfulness can significantly alleviate any stress. What is the saying? 'Prevention is better than cure'.

Humans are mamals, we are social creatures and as such we search for family and community connections. As children the Mother Child bond was our first introduction into this social connection and it was here we experienced loving bonds and unconditional love. This is the ideal scenario we speak of here, quite often as not there are different stories, however for this process we aim to look at a functional bonding process.

Unconditional love experienced leads to feelings of positively re-enforced emotions. A loving, nurturing environment allowed us to function from our natural state. This included face to face contact with mother at an early age, smiling, kisses, hugs, and affection are all interactions that keep our stress reactions turned off. Also important are the basic needs of food, shelter and recent research would have us believe that sleep and the benefits are more important than recently known.

When a child is taken away from the Mother or percieves this, the stress system; sympathetic nervous system is turned on, leading to normal states of depression from a sense of loss. When the attachment is reformed the parasympathetic nervous system turns on, this is our natural state.

Symptoms of stress overload usually occurr as stress responses; heart pulpitations, bloating, constipation, stomach ache and monkey mind, restless chatter. We all hold stress in different places which could manifest as beginning symptoms as pain in the kneck, shoulders, lower back, ankles and other places. This is where Mindfulness can help, we start by letting go of pain and reduce the mind chatter (monkey mind).

Our mind is a reflection of our stress levels, the more the chatter the higher the stress and this means our natural resting state has been turned off, so the nervous system is running havoc with our bodies causing the aches and pains, which left to run havoc can lead to illness, disease or chronic stress.

Controlling our minds allows us to recognise symptoms in our body, such as stomach ache, heart pulpitations and other pains. When we are in a natural state illness, pain and negative emotions are better recognised and delt with using simple skills and techniques.

Mindfulness brings about a state of relaxation. Anxiety, depression and nervous tension are all natural states, however left for too long these can turn to chronic stress. The key is being able to return to a natural state, turning off the stress responses.

The more needs that are met such as basic needs; good nutritional food, home as a place to be yourself, rest, sleep and be comfortable inviting friends and family, safety within your work, home and community. When these basic needs are met our natural state of relaxation is enhanced therfore returning to our natural state as our default.

Worry about tomorrow brings about unhealthy responses which distorts and damages brain development over time, as well as damaging social and familial bonds. Behaviour and communication overtime tends to become defensive and reactionary, aggressive even.

Self regulation is at the heart of controling anxiety and by using the technique of Mindfulness we begin with the very most basic way to self regulate – Our Breath!

# Maslow's Hierarchy of Needs

*What is this inner strength that enables one to maintain calm in the face of difficulties? It is not the result of external factors, medicines, injections, drugs or alcohol. Nor some kind of external blessing. Inner strength stems from true training of the mind. Dalai Lama*

When we look at Maslow's Hierarchy of Needs we see that in order for an individual to develop fully, their basic needs must be met of physiological needs in order for the development to proceed to the next stage. Maslow's five stages represent in some-way the striving of the individual to attain their full potential, yet it also shows that in order to maintain and develop in a fully functional way a balance of growth is required. If a child senses abandonment, then the need of safety has not been met, this sense will stay with them into adulthood, or until this feeling is looked at in the Sandtray. Only then can the child recognise that this abandoned feeling, no longer serves them and the process of "letting go old wounds" begins.

If at any stage an individual's needs are not met, they will display behaviour to match and the law of attraction will determine 'what you put out, you attract'. I am not worthy of love, I am always alone, I can't make friends, I don't belong and so on. The child's need for love and safety can be temporarily removed because of a divorce, separation or changes in family dynamics.

Individual's behaviour will match that of basic instinct if that physiological need is not met, this will reflect their mental state. It is a good idea to have Maslow's model in mind when looking at a child in Sandplay. Without the basic needs, a child will not be able to develop through the stages of normal childhood development unless given the opportunity in the Sandtray, *"growth forward is in spite of losses and therefore requires courage, will, choice and strength in the individual as well as protection, permission and encouragement from the environment."*

**Maslow's Hierarchy of Needs Model**

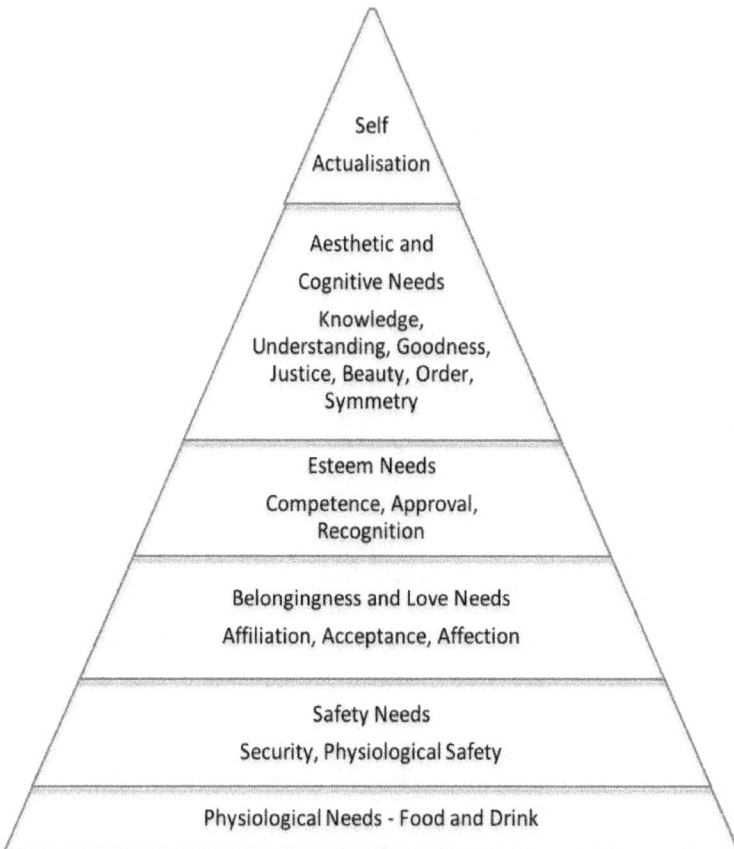

When behaviour is expressed overtly, it is generally a good idea to learn Mindfulness techniques. Prolonged stress seems to dramatically suppress new neuron production, and stress is responsible for the reduction in new growth cells in the hippocampus, the part of the brain that stores long term memory and emotions. Mindfulness can alleviate this type of stress for every man, woman and child, and if children can be taught the Mindfulness technique I have outlined in this book, then all will have the skills to deflect stress when it arises.

Furthermore, when looking at the effects of negative emotions such as anger and behaviour such as hostility on a daily basis it is plain to see how it attributes to higher levels of stress in a child. Humans are approximately 78% water; we have seen how the words can alter the biology. Hostile people are a breeding ground for anger, these individuals display behaviour that leads to temper tantrums, causing unpleasant situations, arguments, negative lifestyle and ultimately anxiety and stress.

What was the seed planted in these children to kick start this behaviour? Imagine if you could nip that in the bud, take the angry man and find the angry boy, the Sandtray would show him where and why he assumed that angry stance; he would see that as a young boy it served him, it was his coping mechanism. Hopefully the Sandtray would also show him that, it no longer serves him as the man. Then it would be interesting to allow him, through Sandplay and Mindfulness to discover his other innate personality traits for him to begin completing his true self-equation.

There are ways of managing emotional responses; through exercise the brain can be stimulated into growth and activity, plasticity. Other ways of managing emotional responses are Mindfulness Relaxation and Yoga; internal exercise practiced for thousands of years, reduces stress through the bringing about of a peaceful state of mind devoid of all self-talk. Yoga exercise is combining body, mind and existentialism, using this method of exercise allows children to work slowly purposefully through external and internal issues. Sandplay is a useful method in controlling stress and anxiety, which takes the child directly to the unconscious memory, opening up memory recall, and allowing the development, as set out by Maslow's Hierarchy of Needs, to activate for the healing to take on a more significant profound direction toward good health, wellbeing and self-actualisation.

In other words, life is a constant searching and exploring our level of personal development. As parents we are the role models, so if we are unable to attain our states, then we disadvantage our children. This is how the patterns are passed on, so it is in every bodies interest that each and every parent, grandparent, uncle, aunty and carer be on a continuous cycle of self-evolvement.

Do you have a purpose and meaning in life, are you passionate about what you do, do you like who you are, how you act, the thoughts you think? Reflect now and sit for a moment and pause, ponder the above questions and if the urge arises start writing down the answers to these questions. If you dare bring the subjects up around the dinner table, or with friends, you may even find that it is not just you who is pondering some of life's existential questions. Who am I, what is my purpose?

*Every day in every way strive to be better and better for this will lead you towards self-actualization.*

# The Benefits of Tapping into Emotional Intelligence

---

*There are hundreds of studies showing that how parents treat their children – whether with harsh discipline or empathic understanding, with indifference or warmth – has deep and lasting consequences for the child's emotional life.*

*Daniel Goleman*

---

What is emotional intelligence (EQ) and why is it important to tap into emotional intelligences? Throughout this book we have talked about self-equation, Polarity of Balance, beliefs, patterns and perspectives. The emotional intelligence of the child is the bridge that connects emotions to intellect, how they understand, why they feel the way they do what they do and how their mind can organise their emotion into an action. Did you know that EQ can be measured by 9 different types of intelligences?

These intelligences when looking at Gardener's Model of multiple intelligences are:

- Linguistic

- Logical – Mathematical

- Spatial

- Musical

- Kinaesthetic

- Interpersonal

- Intrapersonal

- Naturalistic

- Existential

Linguistic is your ability to communicate using other languages.

Logical – mathematical is the ability to solve problems.

Spatial is the ability to use the space around you as would a dancer.

Musical is the ability to tune into the vibrations of the musical resonant.

Kinaesthetic learners prefer to be involved in activities needing to apply    the information.

Interpersonal is the ability to have a good outside communication.

Intrapersonal is the ability to have a healthy internal dialogue with self.

Existential asks the big questions – who am I, what is my purpose in life?


Howard Gardner's multiple intelligences can be used to define, "*a psychobiological potential to solve problems.*" In simple terms this means tapping into your intuitive senses using one or more of the intelligences your child owns, to help solve all manner of problems. Sandplay Technique is the process of connecting to your deep held emotions that were stored as a memory, being able to utilise your strength of emotional intelligence as an integral part of the process of solving problems, enables you to quickly tap into the unconscious. This area is particularly useful for older children who think they have no abilities. Emotional intelligences can also be seen as practical skills; those in touch with their own emotions bring a sense of self awareness and balance into their everyday living and decision making.

A balance of emotions using intellect serves to help manage emotions, so that you allow yourself to be angry at the appropriate moment. In children, we see them having tantrums as a result of being unable to gain attention, perform a required task, unable to voice an opinion. These are all normal states, a child who is constantly being angry because mum said no (for whatever reason), is not an appropriate emotional response. This child is learning to react rather than become resilient.

A part of resilience is the act of self mastery, the building of muscle. A child who learns that, 'no means no', learns to manage his or her emotional state, this brings about a balance, lowers anxiety and enables the child to experience true emotions when and if they are needed. It also serves them in recognising emotions in others, this relates to empathy which is the fundamental skill or emotional intelligence that you would want any person to possess.

Using empathy in all manner of situations, as a form of communication, allows children and adults to manage their emotions which in turn creates a better balance around relationships with self and others. Remember we spoke about sitting around the dinner table communicating. As a parent you can ascertain what intelligences your child possesses and play to those strengths. It will be hard at first, however once you know about the extra intelligences they have it serves to better communication styles, especially once the children reach adolescents. In this stage we can steer our children towards the groups that will give them the most benefits; no good sending our logical, mathematical young person out onto the football field, when they'd rather be doing a gaming programing workshop!

By being in touch with our emotional intelligences, whatever they may be, the Sandplay Technique is a much more rewarding experience, bringing forth self-awareness the child's unique personality traits can be tapped into. They may be very highly intelligent in the Kinaesthetic and Intrapersonal intelligences in which case, this child will be able to go into the Sandtray and by simply moving the pieces around and telling themselves an internal story, they quickly grasp the concept of healing wounds from the past.

Benefits of tapping into emotional intelligences are the strengthening of the child's resilience, by allowing them to tap into innate abilities to resolve conflicts, they build muscle around strengths. The knock on effect of this is gaining a positive self, becoming more optimistic, aware, psychologically healthy, stronger wellbeing and children with a good Polarity of Balance.

I remember my eldest daughter, whom is now my business partner, when she was finishing year 12 and had no idea what direction she wanted to go in with further study or working. I suggested she do the Emotional Intelligence quiz online. The free quiz highlights all the intelligences and gives you the results in a clear formatted version sequencing the highest strengths to lesser strengths or intelligences.

The moment she hit the enter button it was an exciting moment for both of us, I of course knew her strengths well, but of course seeing them in black and white opened new doors and thinking for her. It was a delight to see my daughter be encouraged by the fact that her top intelligence by far was Interpersonal communication. She went on to study management, accomplished roles of leadership with confidence, travelled Europe and make the decision that she had all the skills now to be a great business development manager, keynote speaker and trainer, she is 21.

Building the Sandcastles of Life

Fiona Werle

# *Resistance & Resilience Towards Personal Development*

---

*One is enriched through unfortunate events;
however, they will lead you to the middle
path.*

*I Ching*

---

Resistance is like roadblocks, any blockages that stop a person from seeing the real issue are seen as a resistance. Resistance comes in many shapes and forms, verbal and non-verbal. A resistant child will avoid seeing the obvious blame others or even tells you, "You don't know what you are talking about". Younger children will tantrum, scream and at times become violent. Resistance has many faces; it is a natural part of our development and as the I Ching says, how can we know which path to take if we haven't travelled them all. The important thing to remember around our children showing resistance is that it is a coping mechanism, they are probably mirroring your patterns.

Don't be discouraged, the Sandtray can highlight where those patterns originated and why, remembering children inherit parents behaviour. Resistance is talking to an aspect of the child's psyche, and the mere fact there is resistance, means that there is a button being pushed and development is happening. I have said many times in this book, there should be no blame, we have all done the best we could at the time, parenting is a vast ocean, how we sail the boat in one area may not work in another part. There are under currents, unfamiliar territory and we can never quite know the depths, what we do need are good life skills.

Children in Sandplay will choose figurines and the movements in the Sandtray is their inner child working things out, setting things straight, putting solutions to problems. The ability to release in this manner, can ease tension of which was building up and could have taken on the form of negative anxiety. Another great area to build muscle around resistance is a conversation around the dinner table.

Human development evolves over a life-span, to know and understand childhood is to know a part of self, for the person you are today. In our stages of development whether physical, cognitive or psychosocial we develop the capacity to change. As for any other issues that have buried deep in the unconscious, Sandplay enables children and adults to take a closer look at these deep hurts, pains, traumas and the wounded child's ego buried deep. This burying serves two purposes, first it acts as the coping mechanism and secondly it enabled the child to push away the pain.

The process of self-discovery is a profound one, often times emotional and left with a feeling of being drained of all energy, yet with this emptying out a place for new vitality arises. So resistance is simply put part of our life's process, we all do it. Going back now to the dinner table, imagine as an adult, if you could be authentic enough to talk about your day and the different moments at which you showed resistance. Your child may not understand at the time, but what we do best as parents is plant seeds.

The adults Polarity of Balance emerges through movements in the self-equation, these movements came about as a result of our awareness around our own resistance, shifting awareness is the gentle interaction with our own inner child. This is the key to self-development. With others a more obvious shift propels the self-growth forward, we've all known of someone who has appeared to change overnight, this is an awakening, an awareness or an epiphany. It is important to remember that as the parent you are the role model, you are holding the space and each child will resolve their issues in their own unique way. There is no right or wrong process, only process.

Resistance, roadblocks, rumination and resentment and unfortunate events, are all a part of the equation leading towards resilience. Resilience means to build muscle around the processes that one must engage in, in order to go through the life stages of development. Go back and have a look at Erikson's model, is your child's development on track are they in between or have they fallen in their development.

In order to become resilient, we need to experience the polarities of balance in the self-equation, and as we have said, this means to experience self, touching the realms of the polar opposite, life and death, bully or bullying, losing your voice, finding your voice, trust mistrust and all the other shadow sides that are affecting the decisions we make.

The outcome of experiencing the polar opposites leads to feelings of accomplishment, achievement and acceptance, yet you cannot attain these states unless you have genuinely built the muscle of resilience. You can't always be there to stop kids falling, but you can be there to pick them up, dust them off and send them on their way again. This allows them to experience the fall, feel the pain, it shows them they are loved and nurtured and there is enough trust to let them go, perhaps to do it all over again. Building resilience is feeling the pain, getting hurt, feeling sad, losing friends, falling over, being alone, they are a rite of passage and healthy experiences to have.

Our minds are very clever, they don't let us get away with much, so we can fake resilience, but the minute we need a bit of muscle in order to cope we collapse, because we haven't built up our resilience yet!

Take John, he's 19 working in a job he doesn't really like, however he is doing part-time study because he knows that in order to change he must gain knowledge, have focus, direction and the necessary qualifications. But it wasn't always the case for John, when he was in high school John knew it all, he thought the teaches were idiots that school was a waste of time and after nearly reaching the end of year 10 John decided that finishing school was also a waste of time.

John showed a huge resistance and he inadvertently placed roadblocks every step of the way. When he went out into the world he found it hard to get a job, he still had an attitude and he became quite angry. He would lay awake at night thinking about all the people who let him down; his parents, his teachers, his boss, everybody or so he thought. He would lay awake at night and ruminate!

Through the Sandplay Technique John was able to see that he had adopted the patterns and beliefs of his own father who had been a talented student, however due to family circumstances he had left school early to take on an apprenticeship where he stayed unhappily. He confessed to John that he would have liked to have gone to university to have studied a similar subject to what John was now studying and that he was proud of his son.

John has built muscle, he is able to look back and see what he has accomplished and he looks forward every day to what he can achieve especially in his new found love of learning. John has accepted the fact that he needed to have this life experience in order to get him to where he is today. John has built up his resilience, it was only through experiencing the extreme end of the polarities that he was able to make the conscious decision to make changes, to learn, to grow and take the reins of his own destiny.

John has showed true resilience and sometimes as parents we need to allow our children to make mistakes, because this is their life equation and each and every step leads them towards self-growth, and our job is one of letting go of allowing this process, but yet holding the space at the same time. This is why it is very important to be a constant parent, to guide them in early childhood through the stages of development and to be open as a parent, that we do imprint patterns of belief onto our children. On this there should be no judgement, it is our human culture, our perceptions should be that we always have a choice about how we feel, we create our own emotional destiny according to the way we think and perceive our world.

# How Age Makes No difference in the Developmental Stages

*Why think about tomorrow when all that matters is how we are today. Be well today and the past will be well, be well today and tomorrow will look promising.*

This story is to highlight that the age of a person makes little difference to who we are on the inside. Many of us will look at our children and remember how it was looking up at our parents and now suddenly we are the parents and the same goes for grandparents. Nobody changes on the inside. By this I mean our essence remains the same from birth to death. Why do we talk about this, because I want to highlight the importance of self-development, this crucial area when we look at Erikson's model of psychosocial stages of development age 60+. How is this relevant to a child? As we pointed out, the child becomes the parent who then becomes the grandparent.

If there are issues from early childhood development that have not been resolved, then these issues are carried with us until the day we die. If one looks back on life with few regrets and feels personally worth-while, ego integrity results. Failure to achieve ego integrity can lead to feelings of despair, hopelessness, guilt, resentment and self-rejection.

Therefore, the story of Jasmine a mature age woman can

be the future scenario of someone who has not satisfactorily completed a developmental stage. Failure to fully develop means that themes can recur even into this late stage of aging. Age is no barrier to repeating our parent's patterns.

Jasmine, a mature age woman has an issue with her current husband in that she feels frustrated within their relationship. This is the third marriage for Jasmine and the couple have been married now for one year, the honeymoon period is over. The couple are in conflict and problems are arising as each one learns to adapt to each other's differences. Jasmine and Tony (her husband), are tied into a business together where she does all the bookwork and financials while Tony does the labouring and management of staff. Health issues are affecting both couples; Jasmine has chronic back pain, but feels she needs to put her attention on to Tony who is suffering from a heart problem. Tony recently spent some weeks in hospital with this complaint. They are both grandparents and recent empty nesters.

Viewing individuals within the context of the larger family system with development heavily influenced by evolutionary history, read here inherited patterns, and interactions between biology and the environment is another way of saying, I wonder what type of parenting Jasmine had, and did she have a Mother Bond Connection? When we look at Erikson's Model age 60 + we see if a stage has not been completed this results in feelings of despair, hopelessness, guilt, resentment and self-rejection.

We look at Erikson's Model age 3 – 6, Initiative v's Guilt. *The basic task is to achieve a sense of competence and initiative, given freedom to select personally meaningful activities; child tends to develop a positive view of self and follows through on activities. If the child is not allowed to make their own decisions, they tend to develop guilt over taking initiative, they refrain from taking an active stance and allow others to choose for them.* So that answers our question about Jasmine, at the ages of 3 – 6 she did not properly complete her childhood stage of development and is still enacting out the feelings associated with this stage, in other words she is allowing her inner child of 3- 6 to determine her actions.

Had she been given the tools to build resilience around this stage of development then her story may have read very different. It is never too late, however to become aware of our behaviour and associate it to inherited patterns, then go out and find our true authentic self, or perhaps as a Sandplay therapist I should say, go within.

There are two minds, the rational and the emotional, the thinking mind and the feeling mind. Jasmine's IQ is 120, this is quite a high score and indicates a high level of intelligence. Logical-mathematical intelligence as described by Gardener is a series of complementary intelligences working together. Jasmine's other intelligence stated as the biggest strength was existential intelligence, she is a practicing clairvoyant. "Tony questions my insights, knowing who I am and my abilities". Jasmine cannot act on her intuition; she has developed guilt around this area as well. We see here she is living at either end of the polarity, there seems to be no balance.

Another frustration of Jasmines is Tony's unequal level of intelligence to hers; however, she says "his other intelligences make up for this shortfall". Jasmine feels that she and Tony have very different minds. Gardner suggests that these differences can cause problems in a relationship unless an alignment of thinking is met, if not this situation could lead to a separation. Jasmine says, "There is change; I'm not a wife anymore I feel like a carer. I don't react; I don't say anything as I don't want to hurt him, our relationship has become complacent, I just feel like a carer not a married couple". Jasmine is searching for attention and recognition. Could this be a pattern that is re-immerging from childhood? Remember the age 3 - 6 was all about the basic task to achieve a sense of competence and initiative given freedom to select personally meaningful activities; child tends to develop a positive view of self and follows through on activities.

Jasmine's frustrations are a part of the relationship-equation and Tony's inability to acknowledge Jasmine's role as carer inhibits her to fully live this role. Jasmine was asked questions relating to her own parents, she said that her childhood family structure was both stable and unstable. When questioned about this she said that her father was an alcoholic and her mother a strong woman who kept the family together. Her own mother was unable to achieve a sense of competence and initiative, her freedom was taken away and she learned to cope as best she could with a husband who was an alcoholic, this took away her choice to select personally meaningful activities. It appears that Jasmine is role modelling her mother, confirming that marital and parent-child relationships are interrelated.

Changes can arise at any level of the family system and a change at one level can stimulate further change in individuals, relationships, and the whole family system, and this can be either functional or non-functional. Both parents are influential in a child's behaviour and development, if the parents have a positive relationship children benefit, if they have a conflicted or unstable relationship then the areas affected for the child can be socialisation skills and responding.

Positive parenting enables children to explore their world in its entirety, and whether the child is from a separated marriage, a mixed marriage, extended family, it makes no difference. The stages of development do not depend on the child being part of a nuclear family as a traditional type of family structure, development depends on the ability of the focused family structure to allow the child to develop in the most natural and organic way, allowing the child to tap into their own intuition, to feel a positive bond and unconditional love.

The next sand picture is a great example of How Age Makes No difference in the Developmental Stages. This woman was able to tap into her unconscious and relive her stage of development as age 3-6 Initiative v's Guilt. Unlike Jasmine this woman at the age of 42 and with the help of Sandplay Technique, has allowed herself to tap into her initiative. Her story included her losing her voice at the age of 4, and her ability to speak up, speak out and be heard was disabled. The young child felt a constant sense of guilt which drove her to become a silent meek introvert. All the characteristics of which are not her true authentic traits, therefore her internal environment was fueled by inauthentic and negative emotions and her emotional intelligences were untapped springs.

However, she has managed to change all that, she has turned her energy into a more balanced ratio, she has found her voice, and she has discovered that she is quite a chatty person who enjoys the company of others. Also as we see in the sand picture she has been able to tap into her shadow, the elephant has its trunk up ready to charge, indicating that she will no longer be walked over. The owl represents her wisdom and knowledge and the other symbols represent her fun side, her cheeky humour and wit. As she climbs the tree of life her learned behaviours are intertwined with her innate characteristics, she has found that her strengths and guilt no longer serves her. This woman now sees the numerous possibilities around her of which she can be a part and show a new initiative.

Children often feel a sense of helplessness, that they have no choice, no ability to change, as we have seen this is nonsense. Positive parenting helps in changing their thinking and behaviour which gives them choice, a new perspective. Choice opens up a new energy, it gives children permission to view issues from a wider lens, even if children are not conscious of this process, it allows them to soften, to forgive those who were responsible for creating a sad memory, opening up to seeing a new or different perspective on life is empowering, no matter what age.

This woman at age 42 was able to go back to ages 6 (count the crystals) to complete stages of development in the life cycle.

Take your journey to the centre of your being, take a look at your self-equation and ponder the symbols required to solving or advancing the equation. Using a holistic approach, opening your mind to interact with the inner psyche, being your own geologist will allow you to enhance your senses. Exploration then takes on a new deeper and fuller meaning. Each and every step takes you closer and closer to your true authentic self.

# *The Journey to Our Inner Self*

---

*If we are all human beings, what is the*
*difference between you and me? I think there*
*is a great difference. You are you and I am*
*me! Dalai Lama*

---

Life is a journey – a journey to the centre of our core.
Perhaps Jules Vern had taken his journey before he wrote his
book, "*Journey to the Centre of the Earth*". A German geologist
born in the 1860's, who's passion for minerals, crystals and
ancient wisdom lead him to discovering an ancient parchment,
held within an ancient manuscript. This parchment was from the
12th century, written in the Runic characters of the Norwegian
God Odin, contained the story of a Norwegian Prince who rules
Islandia. What did the letters on the parchment mean, why were
these symbols written in a different style to the manuscript, and
how could these symbols be deciphered? And so began the
equation; from the symbols, letters were formed, from the letters
words were formed, from the words sentences were made and
from the sentences the story unfolded. So began the journey to the
centre of the earth, this could be a metaphor for how our own life
stories begin.

Our world is filled with symbols such as found on ancient
parchments, in caves, books, music and in nature itself. Our
psyche holds the archetypes; the hero, heroin, warrior, prince,
princess, scribe or composer. We are accumulating stories every

moment of the day and working with the symbols and their deeper meanings, which determines language used, which determines our thinking, which sets our brain patterns into neural pathways which then becomes our story, our reality!

Symbols in the Sandtray can invoke the memory of our early childhood, good, bad or otherwise. The way we so intricately stored memories and when faced by certain people, places, times, scenarios, and fears, created memory recall of that moment. This memory became a part of our default thinking which fired up that particular neural pathway. It could have been Uncle John always has a prickly beard and your memory associates Uncle John with that feeling of prickles against your skin. What fires together, wires together, and the more you revert to your normal thinking, Uncle John has a prickly beard, the more you strengthen the pathway or circuitry about that belief about the prickly beard. So what you do by changing your story and memory recall is ultimately creating new neural pathways. Uncle John used to have a prickly beard, but now he is clean shaven. The prickly beard made me feel uncomfortable, but now I feel safe around him.

The child's inner core is surrounded by their own personal symbols and archetypes, releasing dysfunctional memories that no longer serve a purpose allows children to make room for new thinking and behaviour. Tapping into the symbols that give rise to a higher purpose is what Sandplay Technique can achieve. As we have seen, there is a need to see the shadow side, children need to experience the deepest emotions that reside in what they fear, what triggers their anger and in this process they are able to take the journey to their inner core to reveal their true authentic self.

Trauma creates self-sabotaging beliefs and those negative perceptions interfere in our daily functioning. So my observation is this: before we go out to try and change the world, we must first look inward to change ourselves. Then, by changing our beliefs, we shift the energy and the butterfly effect helps to change the world.

Complex trauma is abuse that children carry with them

and they live their life through this memory. Complex trauma is developmental trauma, so these children didn't have the opportunity to go through normal early childhood development as set out in Erikson's psychosocial model. They experienced abnormal development and learnt to live their lives in manic states, which can result in long-term disease, disability, chronic social problems and negative anxiety. Also to factor in, is intergenerational transmission, passing on the defective signals to the next generation, Jung may call this the collective consciousness. This is what we are looking at in understanding how trauma is stored in the cells. Often an issue is outside of the understanding of the family unit because it was experienced by another generation. This could have been living in a war zone, natural disaster or extreme poverty.

Looking closer at this intergenerational transmission of abuse we can see how each generation has coped using; silence, depression, suicide, substance abuse, etc. When early attachment bonds in early childhood are not developed the messages received are of feeling unsafe and not knowing your physical boundaries. Quite often an abused child will grow up to be an abuser him or herself, this is the tragedy of intergenerational transmissions. We saw that the child who has been bullied will turn into the bully as a coping mechanism.

Changing behaviours are neural networks sparking up new pathways in the brain plasticity. Once it's understood that change is possible, then you can help the child to change their thinking and the mind will take care of the rest. In the case of an adult, we want the inner child to be able to say, I don't deserve to be treated like this, I am worthy.

For a child who is still in trauma, we are able to show them symbols, archetypes, shadow and every aspect playing a part in the development. In so doing we can allow some deep healing towards giving the child permission to live their true and full potential and not be guided by their parents' dysfunctional beliefs or the trauma. That's how you add and subtract from your self-equation.

I had to ponder the Australian Indigenous Aboriginals when I was learning about systemic abuse, the repercussions, the intergenerational impact, the stigmas and the sad state of our understanding as a community and individuals towards those that seem to appear less fortunate than us, those who had babies, infants and young children taken from them, lands taken, human rights ignored. A whole race affected by induced trauma. How have they coped?

There is hope though; Dr Bruce Lipton the author of *The Biology of Belief* has done some ground-breaking work in the field of new biology or epigenetics. His experiments have examined the way in which cells process information. Remembering all our memories are stored in our cells in our body. The implications of this research radically changes our understanding of life, it shows that genes (DNA) do not control our biology; that instead DNA is controlled by signals from outside the cell, including the energetic messages emanating from our positive and negative thoughts, how and what we think about. The power of our mind can heal, change beliefs and release stored patterns inherited from parents, grandparents and forefathers/mothers.

This is the sum of the self-equation, and you can see here the direct correlations with symbols and how therapy can work at this deep cellular level to shift some traumatic memories from the cells to our conscious state of awareness. The sand picture can highlight this awareness around an event that was traumatic and allow the child to process this experience and have a new narrative around the experience, or put simply create a new story.

Dr. Lipton's research in cell biology and quantum physics shows that our bodies can change as we retrain our thinking, plasticity. This has vast implications for those who simply are resigned to the fact that illnesses can be passed on in the family. This fact is not true, if you have an illness it has manifested as a result of your own self-equation, there was a trigger, this sits within your self-equation. Change your thinking, change your story and you change the outcome.

Epigenetics has made it clear that there is no escaping that the truth lies within our very deepest self. Individual strengths and weaknesses, characteristics directly attributable to familial and cultural perceptions are programmed into our minds before the age of 6. In turn if these characteristics are not a part of the true authentic self, then these perceptions are responsible for physical and mental health issues experienced in our adult lives. You could say that this is an energetic mismatch, we have taken on the energy of another and in so doing the effects could be living our life through shadow. Turn on your television, watch the news, we see this happening now. How many children never realise their full potential because of dysfunctional programming due to childhood trauma, generational trauma and not fully being able to be themselves.

You cannot run away from your circumstances, you can't hide behind a façade or pretend to be who you are not, you cannot disconnect and you cannot fane ignorance, because every cell in your body holds that memory of the abuse or trauma and you cannot change yourself or future generations until you change your thinking, accept the circumstances and move towards self-growth. Life truly is a journey to the inner self.

*Grief and loss of a young girl searching for purpose and meaning in life*

Fiona Werle

# *Discover Your Purpose and Meaning in Life*

---

*Accept the things to which fate binds you and love the people with whom fate brings you together, but do so with all your heart*

*Marcus Aurelius*

---

When I was young and growing up in rural Australia, my parents and grandparents, uncles and aunties were my role models. They taught me how to behave in relationships and how to communicate using various styles. There was always plenty of laughter, storytelling, food, drink and big sleepovers. The adults would provoke and argue about politics and religion, their favourite topics. I even remember one night at my uncle's place up in the mountains when the grownups held a séance. This opened my mind to other realms and planted seeds; it also scared the life out of me as a young girl.

Slowly but surely, we all grew up. The family gatherings got smaller and fewer and something changed with the dynamics. No longer did these experiences leave a sense of fulfilment: bitterness had crept into the relationships. The conversations took on a passive aggressive form, a negative seed had found its way into the very core of the communication style and not just verbally, most obvious to me were the non-verbals, the looks of disappointment, the frowning, head nodding in disapproval.

The humour was replaced by bitching, whining, disagreement, debate turned to bitter fights. The negative to positive interactions were dangerously out of balance and were affecting everyone's wellbeing. Sad really, it was like watching the destruction of a great empire fall. My parents carried this destructive force into their relationship creating a weakening force field seen and felt on all fronts. Therefore, not only did this force affect each of the families, it also had the consequence of taking from us the sense of community which we had experienced as an extended family.

Upon reflection I wonder whether this influenced my rather lonesome childhood and young adulthood. I know my meaning making as a young adult was quite dysfunctional, which in turn affected my communication style, which was rather negative in all aspects. I had few meaningful relationships and those I had were not based on trust or deep friendships. Within relationships and wellbeing people have a deep need for friendships and to be socially connected to others.

In nurturing our positive relationships, we gain one of the most powerful and consistent results of good mental and physical health. People with high quality social connections experience more positive emotions and meaning in life, the ripple effect. On the other side of the coin, no meaning and no purpose attracts the shadow, and experiences are mainly occurring at the opposite polar.

Interestingly, our values and beliefs we inherited from our parents are not always written in stone. Sometimes our parent's behaviours and communication styles can be a good example for us, on how not to be and act. However, this is not a conclusion one comes to overnight. It is a process whereby as a child you become the observer, you can experience social rejection, withdrawal from community and negative inner thoughts, leading to rumination.

This process is one of isolation and unconducive to good psychological wellbeing. However, it is an important part of the individuation process, forming a sense of self identity and building resilience, this involves the process of separation of emotions and intellect of going down the extreme ends of the Polarity of Balance. Within a family of origin equation this enabled me to eventually accept personal responsibility for my own thoughts, feelings, perceptions and my actions.

This road to individuation consists of many elements and the paths are numerous and each individual will have a unique experience in their endeavour to move towards forgiveness, growth and self-development. Once a child, teenager, adolescent or adult is at this stage, the world and your place in it becomes clearer and this allows passions to form, purpose to rise and meaning to evolve.

Existentialism explains our life's development as a series of processes whereby the people, situations and behaviours we experience are all mirror images for us to look deeply upon, contemplate and learn. Asking those valuable questions of why, what is the purpose of this allow life's lessons to bring forth awareness and this awareness leads us to further walk the path to self-growth.

Maslow's Hierarchy of Needs describes the need for individuals to experience basic needs such as food, water and shelter before moving on to the next level of needs; part of our needs are social support, friendship and family. Meeting these needs gives us a sense of belonging, which help us to create our values. Knowing who are your people, your tribe, your place in the wider sense is part of discovering your purpose and meaning.

The self-actualisation refers to the need for personal growth and discovery that is present throughout a person's life, making up our self-equation. In self-actualisation a person comes to find a meaning to life that is important to them, this can be a lifelong quest and it is said in some ancient texts that self-actualisation is a metaphor for death. Best to keep an open mind, never judge, be aware of the invisible forces that can influence our sense of being. Think of death as a beginning, the end of something means the beginning of something new: Ouroboros!

In the end life is a constant building, maintaining or restoring of our relationships. Our inherited or conditioned beliefs and values are questioned, and our meaning to life is influenced by our own personal values and beliefs based on life experience. Other influences help form our meaning, new skills are gained with every workshop, course or personal development program. Perhaps even in this book you have learnt something new or it has sparked your interest to further research. I encourage this!

The definition of meaning, according to Hooyman and Kramer (2006), *finding benefits from experiences to perceive the world and oneself in positive terms, through constructing and maintaining our most basic sense of self. Meaning can be restored, maintained and discovered through telling and listening to stories. This can include social validation for an existing meaning or adopting new meaning by creating value and appreciation in our lives. Existentially speaking, there is no control over life and the forces that bring events upon us; however, we have full control over our values, reactions and the emotional response we integrate into our meaning.*

Poor health or wellbeing gives way to a lighter and better sense of wellbeing when you are living your authentic life. Thoughts are clearer, the new mind recognises more easily any negativity creeping into the system and like a blowfly we swat at it until it dies away. With the passing of negativity, the ratio falls into a more balanced harmony, striving for that Polarity of Balance. Health is a constant in my life, my affirmation being; I wish for good health, wealth and happiness.

Health is an aspect of life that for the majority of people is a given at birth. If all goes well you are born a happy healthy bouncing baby. As the years go on we learn to become our emotions, our thoughts and behaviours and our bodies react by taking in the vibrations of the energies that surround us, and should those energies turn out to be negative then a constant bombardment can turn your physical or psychological wellbeing into sickness. This manifestation affects your health and once good health is taken from you the road back is long and weary.

Yet this is where we also find the meaning making, this is where growth occurs, this is where self-awareness kicks in to lead us to self-actualisation. Abraham Maslow (1943, 1954) stated *that human motivation is based on people seeking fulfilment and change through personal growth.* The growth of self-actualisation refers to the need for personal growth and discovery that is present throughout a person's life, whether we gain this through health, knowledge or simply by living. This can include our self and soul-equation, for Maslow, a person is always "becoming" and never remains static in these terms. In self-actualisation a person comes to find a meaning to life that is important to them, we place this meaning on the Balance of Polarity where the lessons learnt are a part of the movements in the self-equation.

The relationship wheel takes on a new significance when we see that we are made up of parts of our self, family and environment and all the other layers in between, such as our financial circumstances, hobbies, friends and work. If you've never done the relationship wheel, we have included one in this book as a snapshot for your relationships in your life and where you need to place more or less emphasis, and then you join the dots! A fluid rounding of relationships enables the wheel to go round in a motion of balance and ease.

The changing of our perceptions and communication style brings about the awareness of the negativity ratio in our language verbal and non-verbal which holds the key to building positive relationships. Placing less negative emphasis on one aspect can serve to open up movements in others which enables flow. Once we are in flow we attract positive energy to our life, positivity as we have seen creates more positivity and thus new opportunity. Once again we have succeeded in creating movements in the self-equation.

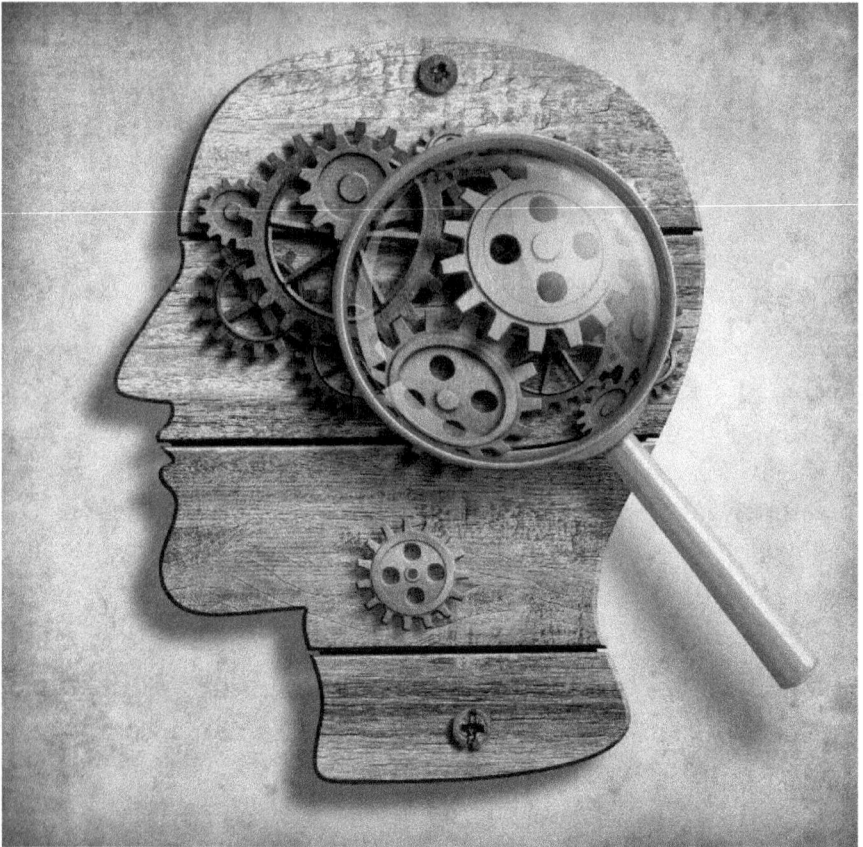

# Relationship Wheel

The wheel changes as we progress through life, nothing is a constant, change happens organically. What is your highest area of strength and which areas do you need to work on? Place the numbers 1- 8 in the sections of the relationship wheel, 1 being the area of your greatest strengths and 8 being the section needing further attention. It is good to go back to this model every 6 months to check for movements.

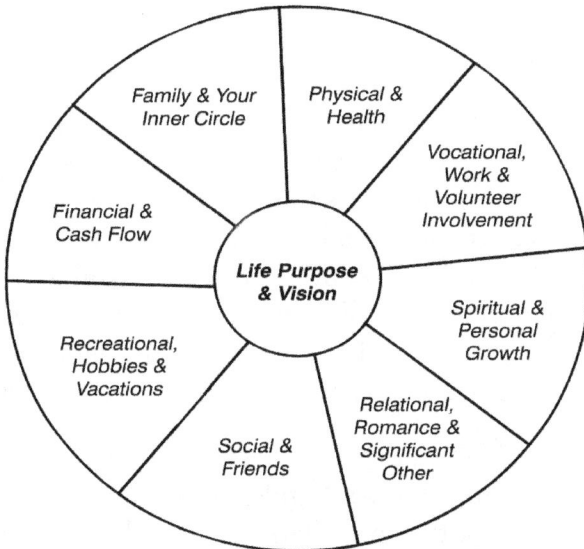

The wheel sections are:

- Family & Your Inner Circle
- Physical & Health
- Vocational, Work & Volunteer Involvement
- Financial & Cash Flow
- Life Purpose & Vision
- Spiritual & Personal Growth
- Recreational, Hobbies & Vacations
- Relational, Romance & Significant Other
- Social & Friends

# *The Role of Mindfulness in Relationships*

---

*Trust in thyself and others will follow*

*Socrates*

---

A reason to integrate Mindfulness into relationships is to activate vital life force into our cells, by sending positive messages through Mindfulness we activate our nervous system, reprogram our unconscious default mode of thinking, plasticity and bring balance to body, mind and soul. Through Mindfulness you create a new self-equation based on your lived experience where you facilitate inner growth and development through love, gratitude and positivity, not feeding your cells fear, hate and stress.

The Mindfulness acts as a sending frequency or holding force that serves to both send and hold thoughts. The sending of thoughts is more akin to affirmations; I am loved, I am worthy, I am healthy, I am capable of success. These subliminal messages eventually turn into new neural pathways. Holding in Mindfulness is the ability to hold the space for this new programming to occur. It is also in the holding that we can train our mind to stop the negative self-chatter known as the monkey mind or rumination.

In today's busy world we forget to stop sometimes and smell the roses. Our intentions are good, but especially for women we tend to place more importance on cleaning the kitchen, making sure the beds are made, floors are clean, washing and then oh its dinner time! Preparing the meal, feeding the animals, getting the kids ready for bed and then do it all over again tomorrow. We aren't very good at letting go of the small stuff. If only we could take a page out of the book of most men, men tend to just stop and take a break when the need arises, they don't carry feelings of guilt around this, and for them they are just taking a break!

So I wonder what seed was planted in our collective female unconsciousness for this to be a division between man and woman. Our urge to have the best looking and feeling home; this is where our family will need to thrive, after all. Can you imagine if in your self-equation your own mother was a hoarder, and the only 'space' you had in the house was your bedroom, you couldn't bring friends home because of the shame, family meals were non-existent because the dining table lay under piles of books, clothes and filth. To get to the laundry was to forge a path over an ever increasing pile of 'stuff'.

You would, as a mother, not want this for your family. A hoarder may attract chaos into their lives; indeed, welcome it in order to put off facing whatever the real issue, this coping mechanism of hoarding hides behind resistance. The Sandtray will uncover this within a short period of time. Breaking these ties of hoarding may well be the soul-equation, freeing the individual to live a meaningful and authentic life. In so doing, keeping the loving bonds with family and releasing the child from the chaos. The Sandtray would tell the story of where the chaos began; it may even give you an age. When the age is determined you are able to ask "and what happened at this time"? The person will know immediately, using further open curious questions they will either put up road blocks or be open to the process.

One technique to start forming a connection with your inner self and therefore bringing you closer to your true self is Mindfulness. We spoke earlier about creating a new set of neural pathways; well this can be achieved through Mindfulness training. What this does is set you up to be fully aware, minding your words; I can do it! Taking the time to 'know thyself' through being in control of the monkey mind, that incessant chatter that can leave you feeling exhausted and awake at night. Imagine being able to control what you thought, when and how! Mastery leads to Mindfulness. Mindfulness can be taught at any age, at any level.

In eight weeks your brain can change! The research supporting this finding is overwhelming. The first technique starts with being in control of your breath. This is the basis for all yogic exercise and is steeped in centuries of practice. The breath is the key. Focus on the breath does a few things, firstly it enables you to start controlling the mind chatter, and secondly it enables you to spend some moments totally immersed in sitting with the self in silence. Here you learn your limitations and find your greatest gifts.

The idea in mastering Mindfulness is to create stillness within your mind, this stillness can allow you to fine tune your pineal gland and so setting up your connection to soul, universal consciousness, God connection, ancestral wisdom; all of which resides within you now, you just need to shut up long enough to listen!

This gift of Mindfulness is the greatest gift to give a child; it will serve them throughout their lifetime. Existential questions are a part of our need to find purpose and meaning in our lives. Reaching a point where these questions are answered can lead to true self-growth, a heightened sense of immortality, greater senses, wider perspectives and a wider colour spectrum from which to choose to see life. Opening a child's mind with Mindfulness serves to open their mind to these larger questions of life which allow them to see their world through a wider lens and encourages learning.

It is in our minds that we make decisions, spring clean friends, come to realisations, see a side of ourselves we had never met, for example accepting the shadow self in Mindfulness, and the impact is far greater especially for a child that suffers from anxiety or depression.

Originally, Mindfulness meditation was brought to America by Madame Blavatsky, who in her own right was a woman light-years ahead of her time. She travelled independently in the 1800's; she lived in India and studied the ancient Indian techniques of healing and wellbeing, which included Mindfulness. Long forgotten and maybe too advanced for the Americans' of the time it lay dormant in the Western psyche, until in the 1970's it was re-introduced by Jon Kabbit Zin.

Although the word Mindfulness would suggest that our minds need to be full, the opposite is true. However, the latter is also true, because in order to fill our minds we must first empty our minds. In the space of this emptiness we tap into the great Akashic Library of Life (this is where a healthy pineal gland is essential) where the resources are innumerable and as invaluable as the air we breathe. The records are an invisible source of knowledge from the collective consciousness of ancient wisdom of archetypal virtues, of a knowledge hidden but not forgotten and carried within our psyche. The more advanced the Mindfulness the deeper into the vaults of the library you travel and the closer you come to the pure essence of ancient wisdom, that archaic whisper heard by some, held by the memory in the environment; the mountains, trees, streams, sacred sites, this is ecopsychology at its best.

Mindfulness begins with the breath, focusing on the breath slows the mind chatter down. The more this is practiced the more practiced you become at quieting the mind. In the stillness, new seeds are planted, positive affirmations can have a place and so begins the journey to knowing yourself.

I have developed a Mindfulness Mediation for children to help relax their bodies and calm their minds. This may be an excellent way to start the day before moving on to learning and education and remember you are both parent, teacher and role model. Your courage lies in the innate connections of spirit, and your heart's desire. So follow your heart, use your intuition and be guided by a higher self. Be mindful of your thoughts because they determine your actions. Check in on self regularly and practice self-nurturing, for if you can nurture self you can nurture others.

<header>
Fiona Werle
</header>

# *Mindfulness Relaxation for Children*

This Mindfulness Relaxation gives the children a complete body mind relaxation experience.

Have the children sit or lie wherever they would like – it may be a favourite spot, have some nice music playing in the background – 432 Hz or Mozart is generally good and easily accessible on CD or YouTube. https://www.youtube.com/watch?v=A7xYccLlO3g

Tell the child it's time to relax their mind from thinking that they are going to do some Mindfulness Relaxation and it will relax their bodies too.

Tell them all they have to do is listen to you, now tell them to close their eyes, take their left thumb (it doesn't matter if they choose left or right) and hold it with their other hand, which they will gently squeeze when breathing in then letting go when breathing out, do it now.

Breathe in gently squeezing your thumb. Breathing out gently letting go.

Now breathe in, gently squeezing your pointer finger, breathing out letting go, now breathe in gently squeezing your middle finger, breathing out letting go, now breathe in gently squeezing your ring finger, breathing out letting go, breathe in gently squeezing your pinkie, breathing out letting go.

Change hands and repeat the process.

Now let your hands rest on your tummy, feeling them rise up and down with each in and out breathe. Count to 5 or 10 breaths with hands on the tummy. Let the children open their eyes and tell them to slowly bring back their attention into the room, wiggle your fingers, now wiggle your toes, now lift your hands up over your head and do a big stretch using your whole body, then relax. Now lie there for a moment and just feel relaxed.

<footer>
121
</footer>

## The Voice of Silence

*Let thy soul lend its ear to every cry of pain*

*As the lotus bares its heart to drink the morning sun*

*Let not the fierce sun dry one tear of pain before thyself has wiped it from the sufferer's eye*

*But let each burning human tear drop*

*On thy heart, and there remain. Nor ever brush it off, until the pain that caused it removed*

*Tis from the bud of renunciation for the self that springeth the sweet fruit*

*Of final liberation*

*Helena Petrovna Blavatsky (1830)*

Fiona Werle

# *The Shrinking World of Culture and our Thinking*

*Life here on earth is but a drop in the ocean
of time, follow the ripples and allow life to
unfold in its natural pattern, be true and
authentic, don't be trapped by dogma, yours
or another's. If you are governed by other's
opinions see them for what they are, it is
'another's opinion, not yours, respect and
honour them as you would expect your
opinion to be respected and honoured*

Our worldview does affect how we behave, experience our world, and interact within our family and social networks. Actually it does much more than that, world views shape individuals, families and communities, setting the scene for a wider perspective, or the butterfly effect, which in turn influences policy makers and those that regulate, co-ordinate rules, regulations and social structure in our Western society today. Worldviews of an individual, group or community form the platform to how they experience everyday life, health and wellness.

To argue that there is a common worldview would be ineffectual, not every individual shares a world view. When we look back at our ancient history we see some countries are termed as third world countries now, however, in centuries gone by they were the hub of industry; Africa was the seat of the ancient gold mining, Egypt was the ruler of the ancient world.

How we view the modern world is influenced by media also, but it is also influenced by our bloodline. Having Hungarian blood on my father's side; any events occurring in Eastern Europe, touches a connection within me, rather than say a tsunami in Indonesia. This is a significant part of the self-equation of which in my case brings in the movements of family and environment. It's not that I don't care about tsunamis in Indonesia and those affected, I just focus more on Europe and events happening there, this is where my radar lies.

Consequently, in order to understand our worldviews, it is necessary to trace back to where views, opinions and perspectives are formed and cultural demographics. Demographic characteristics as part of our self-equation, are the background variables of what helps shape who a person has become. Gender, language, music, age, social circumstances, where and how you live in a country or city, the school you attend and cultural beliefs are all characteristics. The ever changing demographics of cultural shifts bring with it a change in understanding and new ways of looking at things like interpersonal communication.

The world is shrinking, understanding the intricacies of this shrinking world allows you to see that it contains the building blocks of each and every diverse culture and is the key to understanding the perspectives in which diverse groups view and experience the world, through their own unique symbols. This is where the symbols are reawakened, through this cultural chain that keeps the essence of ancient tradition alive. The Indian culture of Hinduism, Chinese New Year, are examples of traditions being played out in our Western streets, filled with the symbols and archetypal energies used in ritual and ceremony i.e. the dragon, fire, princess, colour.

Understanding the symbols enables individuals to build a better and perhaps more complete complex and humane open mind. This then you hopefully take into consideration when in the

Sandplay. Views that your parents' beliefs were once considered cultural, and the alignment with your own are forever present, however, being authentic means you are also creating your own beliefs.

To be mindful of the family equation when working on your own deep unconscious aspects enriches the process, inevitably leading to empathy and a deeper understanding of your old patterning and its roots.

Culture is passed down from generation to generation. This is called the process of enculturation, whereby you learn the culture into which you were born or raised. It is the enculturation that gives individuals, groups and communities their unique ethnic identities. This identity is the platform for beliefs, values and world views. Often times a role model such as parents, teachers, religious leaders and other agencies such as governments, religious groups or media are the main proponents of teaching or passing on culture or extreme views, for better or worse.

Culture itself can be seen as a lifestyle with language, music, symbols, artefacts and ways of behaving, ritual, philosophy, art, laws, religion, communication styles and attitudes, all the symbols that are stored in your memory and all passing from one generation to the next. Valuing diverse cultures allows for perspectives of interested parties to be widened. A widening of perceptions creates an opening to see, taste and hear what is available to experience on a global scale.

Destructive inner conflict, as shadow, because of a sense of lost meaning leads to threats, deception, verbal abuse and sometimes injury or death. It raises stress levels, causing illness and distraction from the problem at hand. This destructive conflict is heightened by the collective consciousness of a country or nation state, experienced in the form of extremism. Although I think Sandplay can also play a huge role in allowing the individual to gain a sense of personality and find their own self-equation, this would depend greatly on many deep held beliefs and the person's willingness to let go.

Interpersonal communication is an emotional intelligence, it is the ability to understand and talk to other people, to ask what motivates them, a capacity to discern and respond appropriately to the moods, temperament, motives and desires of people. It is the key to self-knowledge as here you find access to your own feelings and the ability to discriminate among them and draw upon them to guide your own behaviour.

Quite simply put, those with beliefs different to our own are the ones who will push our buttons the most. An imbalance or low emotional intelligence around this process could result in an inability for movement on the self-equation. An open mind can lead to leaps and bounds in the movements, this is why it is important to teach children to be tolerant of cultural diversity, but understand that some cultural practices are no longer acceptable, and with our wider world view change can be implemented.

Communication is extremely important, understanding what another person is saying and being able to comprehend their meaning through communicating back to them, is part of the fundamental principle of building a relationship and that is what relationships and bonding is all about first and foremost. The ability to communicate and understand where an individual is 'coming from', is called emotional intelligence, the ideal scenario for understanding the culturally different individual in the Sandtray.

*An Aboriginal man is trying to reconnect with his ancestors through the snake as his spirit symbol weapons as symbols represent his innate urge to hunt and support his family.*

# The Impact of Death and Dying using an Alternative Perspective

*The other day upon the stair I saw a man
who wasn't there, he wasn't there again
today, oh how I wish he'd go away.*

*Anon*

Death and dying are a part of life and sometimes when we are dealing with young children and teenagers, death will be a topic that will need to be talked about. At times the only question asked is "why"? I do not have the answer as to why a new born baby is taken from a mother, or why our young ones leave at such a young age. Why do young people die, why are babies stillborn, why are some children burdened with life threatening illnesses before the age of 1, why?

Death and dying in our Western culture is not a subject that we bring up around the dinner table, yet death is imminent! We grieve when grandma or grandpa die or old Uncle Tom who just last month celebrated his 94th. We have an acceptance around old people dying. Our psyche knows this to be the correct cycle of life and death. All is well at the funeral, we shed a tear, feel the loss and then we let it go, as if death were the most natural thing in the world. At the wake we reminisce the life lived, the kids and grandkids talk fondly (or not) of childhood memories, of the silly loving kind things. In general, the experience is non-traumatising.

We know death has no set pattern that we are aware, if we take the knowledge we have gained thus far, a seemingly healthy person can die within a year of being diagnosed with cancer; a beautiful bouncing baby may react to immunisations and be dead within a week. Then there are wars, country against country, drug wars, man against man, violent abuse, man against woman. All these deaths, we sit with in our lounge room and view death as we would an afternoon sitcom; with little attachment or understanding.

It's when the young die, that our every cell in our body reacts. It starts in the pit of our stomach, churning away and flowing up to our heart, then our head to produce the verbal reactions of asking why, why did this have to happen?

*This Sandplay shows how grief and loss may look in the Sandtray*

In my own experience I was able to make sense of the dying process when I discovered The Tibetan Book of the Living and Dying. This helped me to make some sort of sense as to my own brother's death to cancer at the age of 27. For a long time, I walked around asking, why? Why did this young man have to die of such a painful and debilitating disease? As part of my grief and loss healing, I started to take a good hard look at his self-equation.

As we know from the research we inherit 25% from our mother, 25% from our father and 40% from the environment, leaving the 10% as self, seen as our stone or crystal in the sand pictures. As the only boy in the family he was loved, perhaps overindulged, not really encouraged to take risks and explore. Parents fought often, mental illness was present on the mother's side and the father was an Eastern European immigrant who knew the perils of war at a young age.

There was extended family in early childhood, which included its fair share of drama's around the family interactions whether it was the arguments about politics, religion or other family members, there was never a dull moment, but there were obvious underlying currents of family tensions. My brother was sent to a Christian High school where he found Jesus! Symbolically Jesus may have seemed to him to be his savour from the turmoil of a dysfunctional family life. We will come back to this theme later.

At 27 his diagnosis which was first kept a secret by the in-house doctor at Dulux in one of Melbourne's outer suburbs, after seeing his doctor and getting x-rays for his chest pain, he was sacked, no reason was ever given. The reason however became clear when he sought to visit his local GP who sent him for another x-ray some weeks later, only to discover the cancer in his lungs was the size of a grapefruit. In court the original x-ray showed the cancer to be the size of a small orange.

At this time of his life he was heavily integrated into a Pentecostal Sect. He had told his pastor about the cancer who promptly replied "you are the chosen one; the Lord Jesus Christ wants you to be a sacrifice". So it was, that he did nothing, because he believed in his heart that he would die and go to Heaven as the chosen one.

Now although this is a sad story and 27 is too young an age to die, he left this earth believing he had been chosen and therefore death to him was as natural a step in his life equation as was living. However, to those left behind, when the full story was uncovered it brought about feelings of deep hatred, anger, and resentment.

At this point I would like to bring in the ancient concept of Karma, a philosophy from the ancestors of the Eastern orientation. The knowledge is founded on the ideal that our souls chose their life experiences and that these experiences could explain why young babies are still born, or with birth defects, handicaps, mental illness and on it goes. The idea is that our soul, which is our essence, our very inner energy or vibration which resides within our entire body, the main engine room commonly called the third eye or the pineal gland, chooses the type of life and death to be experienced in this lifetime. Karma has its roots in ancient Indian philosophy, Karma is the life/soul experience that didn't manifest in a previous life and must be experienced in this lifetime in order to move onto a different stage of evolvement, rather like we need to experience the different childhood developmental stages in order to experience self-growth in this lifetime.

If this all sounds too far-fetched, put away your current perspectives, take a wander through the ancient world of wisdom and knowledge of which philosophy tells the story and you see the pure form of the soul equation. We look in the ancient wisdom window of knowledge and learn that souls were taken from the earthly plain up to heaven because they had served their purpose. Jesus is the best known figure in western culture, about who stories are told of the ascension to Heaven.

Research has shown that people who practice deep meditation have a strong pineal gland. Taoism teaches that the third eye, also called the mind's eye, is situated between the two physical eyes, and expands up to the middle of the forehead when opened. The third eye is a mystical and esoteric concept referring to an invisible eye which provides perception beyond ordinary sight. In certain dharmic spiritual traditions such as Hinduism, the third eye refers to the *ajna*, or brow chakra. In Theosophy it is related to the pineal gland. The third eye refers to *the gate that leads to inner realms and spaces of higher consciousness.*

In the Tibetan Book of the Living and Dying they talk about the Bardo, whereby the deceased has a period of 40 days after death where the soul now freed of the contains of the body, experiences the life lived over again – soul-equation - and is given the opportunity here to relive moments in time, to either accept or deny decisions made, a sort of test in what was learnt in life and what you did with it. This belief ties into the karmic belief that we are all born to fulfil an experience, whether that was just to be born, to live to the age of 1 or to experience a handicap, all manner of experiences. To explain the death of young babies all they needed from this lifetime was to experience birth, or 9 months' gestation. It is in this period of Bardo that the soul can acknowledge the self-equation and translate it to the soul-equation.

Karma is the harsh reality; that we all chose this lifetime, we chose what we needed to experience in order to add to our equation from this life and perhaps many others, so we chose an early death, or a painful one.

Knowing this allows a part of me to be more accepting of those whose lives have been cut short. It also makes me feel great respect and honour to those mothers and fathers whose babies and children were taken from them. For their burden was an immense one.

In Sandplay Technique we cannot bring back our loved

ones, but we can do two things; we can make sense of our own self-equation and we can honour and respect all those who have played a part in our moments of time. By allowing our unconscious to talk in the Sandtray it shows us the intimate relationship we provided to allow that child, that loved one, to play out their self-equation, because allowing this to form is to allow our own self-equation to process and grow, and ultimately this all adds up to the soul-equation or collective unconsciousness and that's where we are all connected.

# The End as the Beginning

---

*The Self-Equation is made up of the Polarity
of Balance and every experience you have
stored in your memory – Personality, Family
and Environment. Therefore, you are made
up of the Movements in the Self-Equation;
changes are due to Self-Growth and
Development. Awareness leads to the
opening up of memories stored from the past,
when each memory is opened up it leads to
the trail of the Inner Child-Equation.
Ultimately it is this inner child who needs
healing, and as the adult we are capable of
that using love, compassion, gratitude and
empathy.*

---

When my first child was conceived I knew at that very moment I had become pregnant. This very strong connection has stayed between me and my first born ever since. I feel a different connection with each of my children; the love is the same, the connection different and for this I am grateful.

This invisible connection is a strong part of the Mother Child Bond Connection, and how could it be any different when you think about the whole process of creating a life within you, the gestation, the growth, the nine months of holding in your womb, nurturing, the internal dialogue with baby, our hopes, fears, dreams for them and the preparation for the birth itself and the changed environment in which each child is born into.

This truly sacred time can only be fully lived by a mother, a time of deep emotional involvement with another human life. Partners, friends and family can all be included in this adventure, but this is a very special time for the mother who is the creator and holder of life.

Women have been giving birth for hundreds and thousands of years, mostly naturally and with the aid of other women. In my opinion this is how it should stay, women's business. My own birthing processes have been guided by my own inner knowing and intuition. Four home births were a testament to staying calm, focused and in control of the breath; my support networks helping every step of the way, including friends, family, my partner and my midwife - Elisabeth.

I refused to give birth lying down, it was never an option, and I chose the birthing stool, being upright with easy access, so to speak, where I felt empowered and able to control how I wanted the birthing process to evolve. Of course I was lucky enough to have had all my children as home births, which gave me the opportunity to have a Mindfulness Birth. The time leading up to and giving birth in my own bedroom, surrounded by my loved ones felt empowering as a result. No horror stories for me, but I know giving birth is not an easy thing; the pain and contractions can become all consuming, so Mindful Birthing really connects you with being totally in the here and now, it reduces you to the breath, the pain and eventually adding the push, on that last push when the baby's head is out of the passage and scooped up in your arms and placed on the breast, the pain is over and forgotten. But I hear you say, don't gloss over Fiona! True, the stinging, the swelling, the stiches and the bleeding remain, added to this the breasts now become hard like rock melons and the nipples start to ooze the precious colostrum.

Mindfulness breast feeding once again brings us to the pain, the breath and the here and now. Breast feeding is an integral part of our bonding process, here we nurture, feed and hold. For some new mums this process was unable to be experienced, so the holding, eye contact, are as important for the bonding and connection process.

How many sleepless nights and painful wakeful hours are spent as a new mum, and when we are able to sleep we are so captivated by this new life, that we cannot take our eyes off them, we follow their every breath, not wanting to miss a heart-beat, we follow the newborns breath as we listen for life, and all is well.

So on it goes, day by day, we watch to see what colour eyes our baby will have, what colour hair, we are charmed by the way they curl their little fingers around our pinkie, and stroke your breast as they feed. This bonding is the greatest connection that you will have with another human being' this is how you feel the love growing more and more. At times especially late at night when it feels the whole world is asleep, it's just you and your baby. Their scent is more precious than Chanel no. 5, their warmth soothes your soul, and the comfort of them held in your arms your entire reason for existence. At this moment you know your true purpose and meaning to your life.

It is important to remember, that as the child grows, we as parents, are reminded of our flaws and imperfections, we remember that nobody had ever told us that becoming a parent would highlight our need to be authentic, to be true and open and to never pass an opportunity for self-growth. We never knew that our children would push our buttons, be the honest bearers of truth and be the mirror images of how the world sees us. In order to be good parents we need to be good individuals and this means accepting that we all have flaws, a shadow side, questions, perceptions and we are all a large part of where we came from, we all carry the seeds of our parents.

We were all once that baby that was held and loved, and those who missed this part of life still get a second go at unconditional love, this we can give to our self or find it in the relationship bonding with our own newborn, or even our grandchild, this is the greatness of living, of loving, of relationships.

Our minds are great creations, use them wisely, seek help where help is needed, and be open minded to other beliefs, cultures and the invisible world which houses our unconscious, our very centre of who we are and where we came from. Know thyself, for to truly know thyself is to know, forgive and love others.

---

*So make sure to plant good seeds, walk the earth mindfully and always remain open and aware of the subtle energies within yourself and your children, tread lovingly upon our beautiful blue planet.*

---

# *Bibliography*

*Wikipedia*. (2015). Retrieved from Third eye:
https://en.wikipedia.org/wiki/Third_eye

Amigo, J. (1991). The Catalans Mythical Universe. *Dossier*, pp. 10-16. Retrieved
from
htp://www.raco.cat/index.php/Catalonia/article/viewFile/106413/160
690

Aswynn, F. (1998). *Runes & Feminine Powers.* USA: Llewellyn.

Bandura, A. (2002). Social cognitive theory in cultural context. In *Applied
Psychology: An International Review, 51(2),* (pp. 269-290.). Stanford,
USA: Stanford University.

Barlow, D. &. (2012). *Abnormal Psychology. An Intergrative Approach.* Belmont,
CA: Wadsworth, Cengage Learning.

Bee, H. &. (2002). Lifespan development 3rd ed. London: Allyn and Bacon.

*Behaviour Ice-berg*. (2015). Retrieved from
researchmethodsgdansk.files.wordpress.com/2013/03/behavior_iceb
erg_full_120626.jpg: http://ehowton.livejournal.com/447571.html

Cherry, K. (2015). *What Is Brain Plasticity?* Retrieved from About Education:
http://psychology.about.com/od/biopsychology/f/brain-plasticity.htm

Corey, G. (2009). *Theory and Practice of Counseling and Psychotherapy 8th ed.*
Belmont, CA: Thomson Brooks/Cole.

Devereux, P. (1996). *Re-Visioning the Earth. A guide to opening the healing
channels between mind and nature.* New York: Fireside.

*Free Mandala*. (2015). Retrieved from pinterest:
https://www.pinterest.com/pin/391883605048413985/

Gannon, M. (2008). Conceptualizing and perceiving culture. In M. Gannon, *In
Paradoxes of culture and globalization* (pp. (pp. 18-43).). Thousand
Oaks, CA: Sage.

Gardener, H. (2006). *Changing Minds. The art and science of changing our own and other peoples's minds.* Boston: Harvard Business School Publishing.

Gardner, H. (1998). A multiplicity of intelligences. *Scientific American Presents, 9,,* 19-23.

Geldard, D., & Geldard , K. (2009). *Basic Personal Counselling. A training manual for counsellors. 6th edition.* Frenchs Forest NSW: Pearson Education.

Goleman, D. (1995). *Emotional Intelligence. why it can matter more than IQ.* London: Bloomsbury.

Goleman, D. (2003). *Destructive Emotions And how we can overcome them.* London: Bloomsbury.

Health, N. I. (2015). *[[File:Epigenetic mechanisms.jpg|Epigenetic mechanisms]].* Retrieved from wikipedia: https://en.wikipedia.org/wiki/Epigenetics

*How the Brain Creates New Neural Pathways.* (2010). Retrieved from What is Neuroplasticity?: http://www.whatisneuroplasticity.com/pathways.php

Jung, C. (1964). *Man and His Symbols.* New York: Dell.

Jung, C. G. (2009). *The Red Book Liber Novus A Reader's Edition.* London: Norton & Company.

Kalff, D. M. (2003). *Sandplay A Psychotherapeutic Approach to the Psyche.* California: Temenos Press.

Kinser, A. E. (2010). *Motherhood and Feminism.* Seal Press.

Lipton, D. B. (2012). *The Biology of Belief.* Australia: Hay House.

Marohn, S. (2015). *What a Shaman Sees in A Mental Hospital.* Retrieved from The Mind Unleashed: http://themindunleashed.org/2014/08/shaman-sees-mental-hospital.html

Matsumoto, D. &. (2008). *Culture and social behavior, II: Interpersonal and intergroup relations. In Culture and psychology 4th ed.* Belmont, CA: Wadsworth Cengage Learning.

*mindbooster.* (n.d.). Retrieved from http://mindbooster.fr/etonnants-pouvoirs-eau/

O'Brien, C. a. (1985). *Translation of the Sumerian Cuneiform.* Retrieved from The Golden Age Project: http://www.goldenageproject.org.uk/translation_sumerian_cuneiform.php

Peterson, C. C. (2010). *Looking forward through the lifespan: Developmental psychology (5th ed.).* Sydney: Pearson Australia.

Rinpoche, S. (1992). *The tibetan Book of Living and Dying.* London: Random House.

Sheldrake, R. (2015). *Morphic Resonance.* Retrieved from Rupert Sheldrake: http://www.sheldrake.org/research/morphic-resonance

Sigelman, C., & Rider, E. (2012). *Life-Span Human Development.* Belmont, CA: Wadsworth, Cengage Learning.

Sitchin, Z. (1996). *Divine Encounters.* New York: Avon Books.

Thornhill, D. T. (2005). *Thunderbolts of the Gods.* Oregan: Mikamar.

Tolle, E. (2004). *The Power of Now.* Sydney: Hachette Australia.

Tyrer, P. &. (2006, December). *Generalised anxiety disorder.* Retrieved from The Lancet.: http://www.thelancet.com

Van Krieken, R. H. (2010). *Sociology 4th ed.,.* Frenchs Forest, Australia: Pearson.

*What is the origin of the Mandala.* (2015). Retrieved from Innovateus: http://www.innovateus.net/innopedia/what-origin-mandala

# Building the Sandcastles of Life

Training, Workshops and Retreats

- Parenting and Family Relationships

- Learn Sandplay Technique Basics for 3 – 5 year olds

www.sandcastlesoflife.com.au

admin@sandcastlesoflife.com.au

Face Book – Sandcastles of Life

Now Available in the series of Building the Sandcastles of Life, A Therapists & Teachers guide

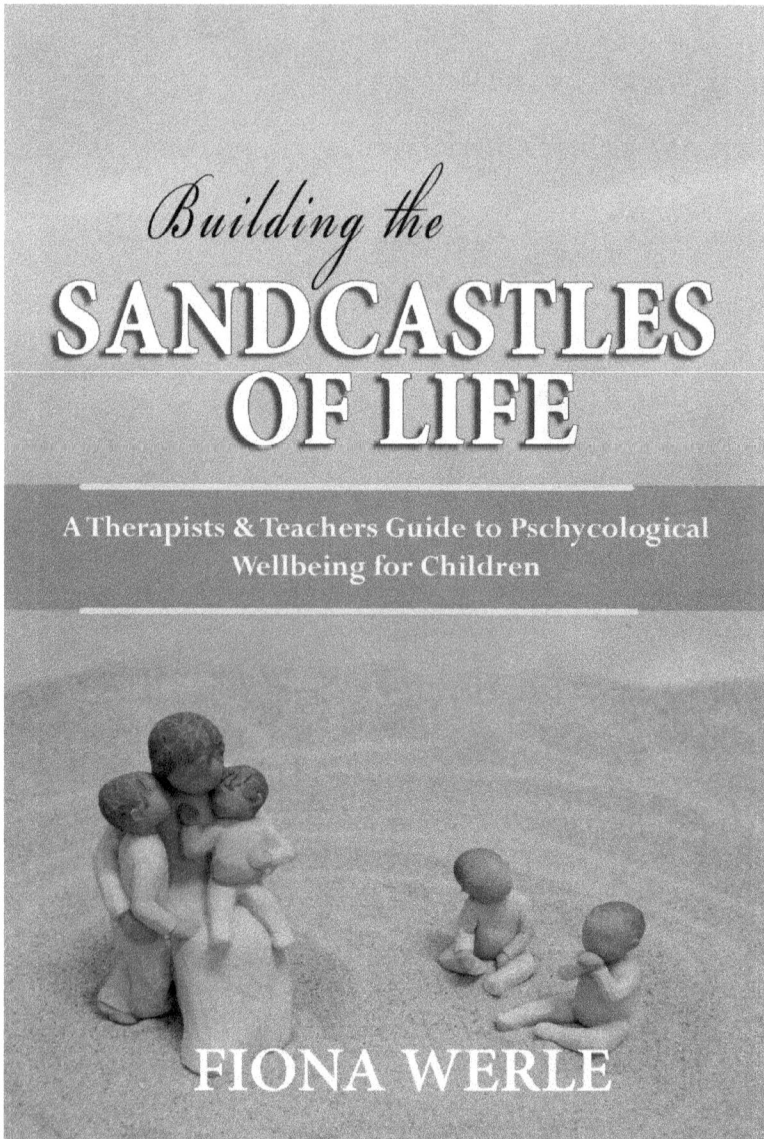

www.ingramcontent.com/pod-product-compliance
Lightning Source LLC
Chambersburg PA
CBHW060759050426
42449CB00008B/1459